REVELATION UPON MY PILLOWS

A Heartfelt Narrative Of One Woman's Struggles

MIA TILLMAN

Revelation Upon My Pillows
Copyright © 2022 by Mia Tillman

All rights reserved. No part of this book may be reproduced or transmitted in any form or by any means without written permission from the author.

Claire Aldin Publications
P.O. Box 453
Southfield, MI 48037

Scriptures marked KJV are taken from the KING JAMES VERSION (KJV) which is in the public domain.

Scripture quotations marked (NLT) are taken from the Holy Bible, New Living Translation, copyright© 1996, 2004, 2007 by Tyndale House Foundation. Used by permission of Tyndale House Publishers, Inc., Carol Stream, IL 60188. All rights reserved.

Library of Congress control number 2021931222

ISBN 978-1-954274-90-7 paperback
ISBN 978-1-954274-91-4 eBook

Printed in the United States of America.

Table of Contents

Acknowledgments 5

Prologue 7

Chapter One: The Early Years 9

Chapter Two: Siblings 37

Chapter Three: Fathers 49

Chapter Four: The Children 59

Chapter Five: Overcoming 97

Chapter Six: Dreams & Visions 139

Chapter Seven: Truth Over Popularity 155

Chapter Eight: Hearing God 167

Chapter Nine: My Testimony 181

Chapter Ten: God Gets the Glory 189

Acknowledgments

Holy Spirit,

Whatever God wants the readers to receive from my life experiences, allow it to come to their minds.

Abba Father,

Be glorified through this book. Speak a personal message to your children. Let them know that nothing they went through has gone unseen. As they endured as good soldiers and have been living sacrifices, remind them that You shall reward them. May they be unmovable and always abounding in faith standing still to see the salvation of the Lord. Through tears in their eyes and heads hung low, through the pain of broken hearts, with the questions of why and even through the rejection, may they trust in You, the God of our salvation. You are the Lord who reigns, the Lily of the Valley, the Bright and Morning Star. You are our Peace and our Protector. God, you will be everything we need when we need You.

Readers,

Call on Jesus. Wait on Him. Trust in Him. Believe in Him. Seek Him. Reach out to Him. Hold on to Him and don't let Him go.

Prologue

Winning a book contest hosted by Claire Aldin Publications is how I started the publishing process of this book. I realized that writing about my experiences may not be popular among those who are on the other end of the story. The intent of this book is not to embarrass or hurt anyone. How could my children understand and distinguish the difference between gossiping and telling your story if I did not set the example? Therefore, I am telling my story and I shall not be ashamed of what others did to me or saw me go through.

Chapter One:

The Early Years

Have you ever dreamed of living in poverty or having low income? Did your life goals consist of being homeless and losing your job? Did you ever find it desirable being a victim of molestation, with domestic violence being the "icing on the cake"? Would you like to be abused mentally, verbally and physically? If you answered no to any of these, I can agree with you that none of these things are desirable to me, either. Yet these are some of the situations I endured for reasons that were either beyond my control or controlled me by my own permission.

Poverty is a place of hardship. Many people still live in poverty. Low income, welfare and subsidized housing are things many people are well accustomed to. How about living in *fear*? Fear of losing someone, a job or a house. Many can relate to learning things, but my fear was to live in poverty and not be able to survive with my children.

Do you know how embarrassing it is to be put into a situation that is out of your control? I grew up poor. I come from a place of struggle living with mice, roaches and bugs. We ate one meal a day that we had to survive off until the next day. We lived each day, not knowing what tomorrow would bring. Living without electricity and relying upon candlelight by night wasn't foreign to me. By day, I occupied my time with reading or playing outside. Winter survival and having no heat consisted of dressing with layers and layers of clothing and placing blankets over the doorways to keep out the cold drafts.

In the past, before the utility company united the electric and gas bills, if the lights were shut off, you could still use the gas stove to heat water or cook. During the winter months, you could heat the house with the oven and cutting on all four stove eyes. I learned how to stay warm by putting hot water in a bottle and putting it between my legs up under a cover to stay warm that way. I learned how to make food stretch by adding water to juice and water to milk. I issued out smaller portions of food and held on to the words that *we eat to live and not be greedy.*

As I think about my struggles, I have many questions of "Why?". *Why did I allow this to happen? Why am I dealing with this? Why am I not strong enough to make a different choice? Why am I so disobedient? Why am I so bound?*

I am the second oldest daughter of four children—two girls and two boys, between my mother and father. The girls are the oldest. Growing up in a two-parent household, I've witnessed my father's drug abuse and abuse toward my mother. Watching such acts of disrespect and my mother's willingness to stay confused me as a child. One would think it was common sense that if someone hurt you, it was not love. Yet, my mom whipped me and told me she did it because she loved me. Therefore, this cycle of hurt and love was embedded in my mind.

We grew up poor and struggling. Although my mom kept a job, her income was insufficient to supply my father's habits *and* provide for us. His habits were fed to keep the peace. Upon feeding my father's habits, Mom was left alone for days which meant we were either left by ourselves, or in the care of our neighbors. My mother battled depression for reasons I didn't realize until I got older.

I stayed after school and did not miss a single day of school because my reward was breakfast and lunch, along with the education. I made sure to stay in my schoolbooks to keep from being focused on the things going on around me and at home. Despite being a straight-A student in elementary and middle school, I do not remember my mom ever telling me that she was proud of me or even coming to support me at events. One time, I was awarded $100 for honor roll in middle school. My mom did not show up for the ceremony, but she was excited about the money. When I asked my mom how she met my dad, she told me that Dad stayed two houses down from her as a teen. She stated my aunt noticed him first and pointed him out to her. One day, Dad approached Mom and told her that he'd been watching her and liked her. Although Mom wasn't interested in him at the time, she hung out with him anyway to keep her mind off her troubles at home. Mom hated that she hooked up with him, but it was better than being at home and under the strict control of her mom and stepdad.

Mom told me that Dad was always into something in the streets. She didn't recall if it was him or his brother who used to curse at their mother; it may had been my father. She married my father, but he was controlling and abusive. When she believed to have control over her life, it was making unwise decisions to sell her body. He never wanted children, yet she did. She wanted someone who would love her unconditionally and felt that unconditional love would come from her children. She said she don't know why things got so hard when we got older. Mom claims to have given us all we ever wanted as children; however, I don't remember that.

When I asked my mom about her real father, she stated that she didn't know much about him except his name and that he was married with a family of his own. My grandmother made an unsuccessful attempt to abort her herself. Being fearful of dying, she decided to keep her. Perhaps my mom was mistreated because she was unwanted.

Growing up in a dysfunctional household, my mom was molested by her stepfather and siblings. Despite all of the wrong my mom dealt with, she still had a genuine heart for people. She tried to keep those around her from feeling lonely. Being a mother of four children, my mom wasn't alone; however, she was lonely and yearned for adult conversation. She yearned to be loved and approved by others.

The molestation could have stopped with my mom if she would have told; nevertheless, it turned into a generational curse that I prayed would not be passed down to my children. Many times, we don't tell out of fear of not being believed or that nothing would be done to the molester. Would telling make matters worse? My mom never told, and my uncle continued the cycle with my mother's daughters.

My childhood memories consisted of neglect and abandonment. I recognized the faces of my dad's company and developed a strong intuition. Whenever I felt something was wrong, I was always told that I was crazy.

I walked upstairs to check on my dad, who was in the bathroom. Then, I heard a knock at the door.

"Who is it?" I asked.

The guy responded with his name. It was my dad's friend who was always over our home. I used to always tell my dad who was at the door; but after getting cursed out for leaving a friend knocking, I learned that if it's his friend, let him in. When I let this man in, he gave me a hug. I told him my dad was in the bathroom.

"Okay, go back in the basement to play," my dad's friend responded. I went back downstairs and after five minutes, I noticed the radio was turned up. Music bumped loudly before it went silent. I went upstairs and noticed that everyone was gone. It wasn't unusual, so I went back in the basement to play.

Fifteen minutes later, my mom started calling for us.

"Who opened the door?!" My mom yelled once we got upstairs.

"Me," I responded. As it turned out, the man visiting my dad actually came there to kill him. As a result, I got a whipping for letting him in and was told to never open the door again. I felt bad for years. Although my dad fought him off, I replayed the "what ifs" in my mind, and that I would've been the reason my dad would have been killed.

Despite my uncle's indiscretions, my mother allowed him to move in with us when I was eight years old. Growing up poor and barely eating, my uncle made things a little easier for my mom. He had money to help, but he also moved in with a drug habit and much worse—a spirit of lust. My uncle molested her, then voluntarily married his stepsister and had two babies by her. He was sick, and I don't think she realized how much. I wonder how people discern the spirits that others carry. Why didn't my mom recognize the spirits in my uncle? *You must be careful of the company you keep and who you allow into your home.*

My uncle owned a huge collection of pornography magazines—thousands of books that, as young children, we should not have had access to. Yet with peaked curiosity, we looked at the magazines. We showed these magazines to our friends and even imitated what we saw. Such exposure opened the door for the spirit of lust with my generation.

By the time I turned nine years old, my uncle was touching me inappropriately. My sister even made me do sexual things to her. Eventually, our neighborhood friends got involved in the debauchery.

In our basement, after showing some of our friends one magazine, a fourteen-year-old boy decided to take my sister and imitate what he'd seen. She was only eleven. At that time, I didn't know what rape was. I had only seen voluntary sex acts.

"No! Stop!" my sister cried. I stood there, watching in shock. He didn't penetrate her, but his simulated acts inflicted pain upon her. I got in trouble, and my sister was mad at me. This confused me because the same "No" I told her when she made me perform oral sex on her was the same "No" she told the fourteen-year-old boy. I didn't know what to think or what to do; however, I knew none of it was right and I did not like it.

My uncle continuously taught us inappropriate things. He would show the naked ladies he made out of aluminum foil. We laughed and giggled about it until he decided his books were not enough. He wanted fresh meat. It first started with him asking to touch my behind. Although I told him no, he was relentless in his pursuits. He begged me daily to touch me, and each time I refused. However, I didn't know at the time that he was already touching my sister.

My uncle told me that my sister *and* my mom allowed him to do such things. Having a soft spot for mom, along with hearing about her "consent," I consented to my uncle touching my behind when he offered a few coins. I felt bad because I didn't like it, but if my sister and my mom allowed it, then who was I to say no? I was the baby girl. I had to follow their example, not to mention how much I wanted to be like my mom. My mom was in nursing school and since I desired to be a nurse, as well, I admired her. I completed her homework and assignments for her because she was dealing with so much. She never completed school, although I helped as much as I could. I wanted the same character of humility that I saw in my mom, but it seems that I took after the naïve side. However, why didn't I confirm what my uncle said with my mom? My uncle said she would be mad about the money part so not to tell her. I believed the hype. Receiving money from him wasn't abnormal because he was Uncle J. So when my mom asked, I would be telling the truth; however, I didn't share *what he did* to give me the money. I still can't believe I was so naïve.

Although we were struggling, we always had a house full of people. We had card parties and some would bring their children and spend the night. We were always left alone to go play in the bedroom. We always found ourselves doing inappropriate things. Since I was a crybaby, I was always the one to be on the lookout. Sometimes I wasn't allowed to play because I wasn't "playing right." I became so fearful of everything that I was the one who my siblings, cousins and friends talked about. Along with being tormented with scary stories, they took advantage of me by sending me to do things nobody wanted to do. I was the one who took whippings for the whole team.

My sister and I never told that we were being touched, so would it ever stop? I don't know, especially since the generational curse trickled down to my uncle's son. Most times, we let things go unsaid because we feel it was just a season. Hoping the person changes once you have that talk. That is not everyone's story. How many people know of those who have molested, raped, beaten and killed? The behavior did not just happen that day. It has been a continuous occurrence.

I was scared of boys because penises scared me. I hated anything that resembled the tip of a penis—hot dogs, polish sausages or Vienna sausages. I always tore the ends off, which would upset my mom because in her eyes, I was wasting food. I would sit at the table, staring at the end of a hot dog while refusing to eat it. I was embarrassed to eat popsicles or even lick ice cream bars and cones. I preferred a bowl of ice cream over an ice cream cone, and whenever I ate a bomb pop,

I would bite it instead of sucking it. Needless to say, my uncle traumatized me.

Along with being afraid of male genitalia, I thought I was gay as a child. When I was nine, a girl who was younger than me would always touch me in my private area. At that time, I knew nothing about sensations. I was always the one being asked to touch someone else. Nevertheless, I was comfortable being around this girl and would always spend the night.

One night, I was awakened by her performing oral sex on me. Although I told her to stop with a questionable look on my face, I could never forget that feeling. By this time, the questions sprinted through my mind. *Am I gay? Where did that feeling come from?* This evoked a yearning and desire for that feeling. As a result, I started touch myself constantly and an addiction formed from that experience. In fact, it is a habit that I still battle with to date. *Why? Help me, Lord. Deliver me, Lord.*

I pray earnestly when I encounter homosexuals. I never judge, and I understand their frame of mind. Some people say they are born that way, and some have always known that they were a girl or boy. They were not born that way naturally. The more they were exposed to it, the more they desired. I was scared of boys for a long time and I clung to girls. Girls were safer to me until I started being touched by them. It was always younger girls, too.

What was going on in my childhood neighborhood? Seemed like everyone were playing the "touching game." What was in me that I was even approached without question? It was as if it was known that I would go along with it without a fight.

As a child, I could not get anything to drink without eating most of my food. No matter how thirsty I am, I can never drink anything unless I had eaten at least half of my food. I can't enjoy my food unless I am reading a book while eating. As an adult, I can enjoy my food without reading since I have been eating and fellowshipping with my best friend, Hope.

At the age of eleven, I got the beating of my life when one of the neighborhood girls' mother caught us touching each other. Much to my embarrassment, not only did my mom whip me, but she told everyone and I was on punishment for a month. I didn't even care. It kept me at peace and by myself. By that time, my uncle had moved out, so I had time to think. I watched television, wrote and did my schoolwork.

A week after it happened, we went to my grandmother's house and I was grilled by my grandmother and aunt. They asked me if I was gay and where did I learn that. I didn't have an answer. I didn't want to say I learned some stuff by being forced. My uncle touched me. Girls in the neighborhood touched me, and I liked it. It's embarrassing, right? To like something that is clearly so wrong. After I gave them no response, I was told to go upstairs.

"You think she seen something? You think anybody messing with her?" I heard my mom ask my aunt. That was my open door to talk to my mom, but I didn't.

At eleven years old, we moved into my childhood neighborhood where I would live from age eleven to age nineteen. The struggle seemed harder as life took a toll on the many situations we were in. At that point, my mother started doing drugs and selling her body. We were left with no food to eat, no gas or electricity in the house. My mother was the type where you did not know her business, yet the walls talked and so did the streets. Going without food happened periodically. There were times when I came home from school and the lights were shut off. I learned to adapt, not knowing what tomorrow would bring.

When I turned twelve, I began to housesit for my auntie. She had bought a fully furnished house. I didn't know my aunt was experimenting with her own sexuality at the time. Whenever I walked into her house alone, I always got an overwhelming feeling to touch myself. I had to find some sort of pornographic movie, but she never had anything around. I frantically looked for a movie with some type of flesh scene so I could masturbate. I was addicted and did not know why.

Afterwards, I felt so horrible and would ball up in a corner, crying. My aunt would come home and ask, "Why are you in the dark all the time?" I prayed as best as I could for help. I couldn't stop touching myself and had no one to help me. My mother was sleeping with men. My aunt was gay for the moment. Such an embarrassing act that people seemed to think was normal. I had people around who would love for girls to touch each other. I'm twelve. Why are grown men lusting after me? Why am I being told they can touch me better? What is this I am struggling with? People says its normal; but why do I feel so bad when I do it?

I began developing physically when I was fourteen. I looked like my mom—more than I cared to believe. I realized just how much I looked like her when her male friends started telling me so in more ways than I cared to hear. My mom even told me that I was "sitting on money" and should never be hungry again. I did not understand what she meant. In my mind, I thought she was telling me that there is greatness inside of me and I would be going places. Never would I imagine that she was telling me to sell myself if I wanted to eat. However, I soon understood what she meant in an embarrassing, yet life-changing turning point in my life.

One day, I followed my sister to a house party. I was fifteen years old, trying to be with the "in crowd," wanting to have fun. My sister and her friend each went to some back room to have sex. Me, being a virgin, was left in a room full of people who I didn't know. I was a good dancer by imitating my sister. The way I moved enticed the guy. Due to everyone else there being sexually active, it was assumed that I, too, was sexually active. People really believe the cliché, "birds of a feather flock together."

I was taken to a back room where I was alone with this guy and no one to protect me. I talked with him and asked questions about his age, etc. He told me that he was nineteen. Then, he hushed me up and talked me into having sex. When he entered me, he said, "Oh, you a virgin," then he got up. Not knowing what happened or why he got up, I called for my sister. My sister and her friend ended up making the guys walk me home. My sister decided I couldn't hang with them again. I didn't like hanging with my sister and didn't want to have sex with strangers.

I started staying at home again and being around my mom. I would rather deal with being hungry or even lonely whenever my mom would leave than deal with having sex. One day, I was in the shower and realized my breasts were leaking. I instantly called for my mom. She slapped me and said, "You're pregnant."

"Huh?" I asked. My sister started smiling and was happy, but I was terrified. I was fifteen. *I can't have a baby.*

What can I do for a baby? I have nothing, and my baby will have nothing. My mom wanted to know who the guy was. I explained to her that I didn't know him, but my sister did. My mother instantly asked if he paid me. She went off, saying I should never give up anything for free. That's when I realized what she meant when she said I was sitting on money. I lied and said the guy gave me twenty dollars, which calmed my mother down.

"Well, at least you got something," she responded.

I was so hurt because for one, I lied; and two, for what was I about to do. We finally got in touch with the guy. It was such an embarrassing moment. I found out he was twenty-two, not nineteen. My mom started telling him he should have known that I was a virgin by the way I moved and that at least he paid me for it. He hollered, saying that he ain't pay me nothing. My mother beat me right there for lying and most of all, for giving it up for free. All the while, she was hollering, saying that I can't even feed myself and here I am, bringing a baby into this world. *My child would not be her responsibility.* That day, in that moment, I vowed that I would take care of my child and give him a better life. I would not do the things my mother did. This was the beginning of me trying to make it out of poverty and out of a poverty mindset.

I've always dreamed big and allowed my imagination to take me away from reality. I told myself I would never be in this situation. I vowed that my children would never have to endure hardship like I did as a child. I would give them all they want and they will not struggle at the hands of my doing.

When I was pregnant with my first son, my sister had got into a disagreement with some girls I knew nothing about. It happened that I had an elective class with my sister, so these girls were following me, talking about they were "the abortion clinic." They wanted to fight me. I asked who they were talking about. They said, "You." Although I was pregnant, I was going to fight. Had no concern for my child.

I believed I would be protecting myself, but what if they hit me in my stomach? She had already threatened me, but my friend pulled me to class. When I sat down, I was visibly upset.

"What's wrong?" my sister asked.

"Nothing," I responded. However, she knew something was wrong. I rarely cried, not in school.

She jumped up and yelled, "Tell me what's wrong!" While she was in my face talking, approximately six girls walked in and said, "There she go." My sister looked up and instantly jumped at them asking what's the problem. The girls backed up and said nothing.

"We thought she was someone else," they said. I was excused to go home because the teacher didn't know what the girl's motive was.

My brother was in a gang. One day while riding home on the bus, some people assumed that since I was his sister, I was in a gang, also. Because I would fight for my brother, he told females he had words with that he would get me to slap them. Now, I liked to fight; but I would only fight if I *had* to. My first priority was school. Coming home from school, a girl who my brother had threatened approached me. She threatened to slap me, but I was unmovable. Since she saw no fear in me, she told this huge guy who was with her to slap me.

He stood over me and rang the bell as I watched him. He stood next to the back door to get off when the bus stopped. He ran back to me and slapped me so hard before exiting the bus. I was nine months pregnant at the time. I tried hard to get up, but my friend held me back while the bus took off. I yelled for the bus driver to stop, but he refused. He would only drop me off at my usual stop.

About six years ago, I saw the girl at a gas station. I was with my ex-husband at the time and I pointed her out. She remembered me by the way she looked at me. I instantly felt mad, but as I stared at her and looked through to her spirit, I saw guilt. She didn't know what my reaction would be, as I had a reputation for fighting.

Why do I love to fight? It came from being bullied and pushed around as a child up to my young adulthood. As a teen, my sister and her friends were always fighting someone. Being her sister, I was considered to be an enemy as well. So, wherever I went, I had to fight just from association to the point that I got used to it. It was how I settled all problems in my early adult life although I truly wasn't solving anything. I would try to resolve the problem by talking first. When that didn't work, I fought.

When my mother finally grew tired of the mental and physical abuse, we set out to find another place to live. At this point, going from poor to poorer was not healthy; yet, it was choice my mother had to make. She chose to be poor and free instead of poor and bound to an abusive relationship with my father. At the time, being poor was normal and everyone around us seemed to be in the same situation. I just looked at life as the hand I was given.

I watched my mom manipulate my grandmother with guilt. My grandmother and my grandfather—my mother's stepfather, molested my mom. My mom never got specific, yet she would say, "the stuff she made me do to her." Whenever we had needs, my mom put on a guilt trip to my grandmother, telling her that she's the reason she acts the way she does. My mom wanted my grandmother to help her more than she did. My grandmother rarely came around; however, when she did, she was bringing something to eat and would always stand outside. She rarely came in the house. I believe she was embarrassed about our living conditions.

During the holidays, we didn't have a car, so we always had to wait on someone to come get us. I wondered why when we got there everyone was on their second helpings or were preparing to leave. We were always the last to leave. It was because nobody wanted to pick us up in the first place, and we didn't get a ride home until the last person was ready to go. I saw the dysfunction and I felt the tension. My mom and her children were just being tolerated.

My schooling served as a coping mechanism from the dysfunction going on at home. I kept my head in the books and participated in extra-curricular activities at school to avoid going home to such a poor environment. I loved my mom, yet it seemed like life had a strong hold on her. So, I began to *dream*.

I loved the school assignments that consisted of me sharing my life goals. I would write such things like, in ten years, I would love to accomplish working toward my dreams. I wanted to become a nurse because I loved helping people. I wanted to be wealthy and live in a large house with my future husband. Also, I wanted to buy my mom a house and take care of her.

This was the plan of an eleven-year-old, and it remained my goal every year. I started working as a teen. Whether it was tutoring after school to make a few dollars or working in the school store, I did whatever I could to make sure I attended activities where I could at least eat. I hated being poor. I would never wish that situation on anyone. I could not afford the things other children had. I could not go to the places or events others went to because I did not have the money. Thank God for some friends who knew my situation yet accepted me anyway.

One friend let me stay at her house. I did her chores because I believed it was better to hurry and get it done so we could play. Yet, I was hungry. They had lights, cable, food and security — all the things we did not have at home. She also had an older brother who had all the neighborhood guys at their house. I was constantly chased for reasons I didn't care to partake in. Knowing I had a loose mother and sister, some assumed that I, too, was loose. I hated the attention I got and that people assumed that what one did, I should do also. My bubbly attitude and cuteness attracted the boys, and my fourteen-year-old friend would have her fun with them. We had many falling outs because I was just her lookout. Her parents trusted us to go places together, and she took me along just so she wouldn't be alone.

When I was fifteen and pregnant with my first son, Uncle J woke me up, pulling on my clothes. I was sleeping on our front room couch during the day. I have no idea how he got in the house. He may had been visiting because it was daylight. This same uncle who molested me as a child said, "You having sex now, so we can go further like your mom let me." Despite being half asleep, one thing I refused to do was to let my uncle rape me or manipulate me into having sex.

"I am you niece—your blood niece," I said to him, looking him directly in his eye. "You are my uncle. You will not touch me, neither desire to touch me. I am telling my mother."

"Okay, tell her but she can't say anything 'cuz she did it," he said before leaving. I told my mom that my uncle wanted to have sex with me and she stated to that J is still on that and he ain't gonna never change. She asked me did he touch me. I said no. She said to stay away from him. That's sad to say the least to be instructed to stay away from your uncle.

We only saw our family around the holidays. I used to be so uncomfortable as a child with my whole family around. It was as if my uncle had a way of looking at me and zoning in on my every move, even with a room full of people. Whenever he could, as I got older, he would corner me coming out the bathroom or the kitchen. If I was coming in the door, he would find a way to mistakenly brush up against me. After I had my baby, he would call me up begging to sleep with me. It was weird and scary. I was being stalked by my uncle. I don't remember at what point it ended, but it did.

In ninth grade, before I got pregnant, I went to go live with my grandmother so I could have easier access to get to school and to avoid conflict with my mother. At that time, we didn't get along due to her lifestyle and my smart mouth. Since my grandmother worked at Martin Luther King High School as a custodian and lived closer to the school, it worked out better for me to stay with her.

My mom lectured me about watching out for my grandfather. She told me that if he even looks at me, to let her know. I only lived with my grandmother for a semester because my grades would not allow me to stay at King High School. I was so unfocused. I could hardly sleep at night. I had night terrors. I thought constantly of what happened to my mom in that very house. Mom described how she would lock the door of the same room I was sleeping in to keep my granddad and uncle out. Every night, I woke up screaming. Whenever my grandmother asked me what was wrong, I would never tell her.

One time, my grandmother told me that I came into her room and asked her a question that made no sense; however, she would not tell me the question. She just asked, "Mia, why did you come in my room last night?" I had no idea. I have been known to sleepwalk. The only time I remember sleepwalking is when a guy who stayed on Mack Avenue at the corner of Nottingham lived upstairs over the laundromat. He called out to me and said, "Help me. I need help. I can't take this. I'm gonna kill myself." I said, "No, here I come." I began to walk to him. He was a good two blocks from my house since we stayed two houses off the corner. I had my night gown on with no shoes. I took off.

After waking up, my mom asked me where was I going at three a.m.? I was like, "Huh? What are you talking about?" She said one of her male friends saw me walking barefoot down the street. When he asked where I was going, I didn't answer. He said I had a blank gaze on my face and I kept walking. She said I was fighting him to get down the street, but he picked me up and brought me home. She said I kept hollering, "I got to help him." I told her that the guy down the street said he was going to kill himself and he needed help. She asked what was I going to do? I said I don't know.

An hour later, the news traveled that the young man committed suicide. I was puzzled and hurt. Why was I the one who heard him? Why did I sleepwalk to try to get to him? I pray to learn how to intercede and pray. I still don't understand a lot. I'm shown things about people and don't know if it is really God or a figment of my imagination. I had a bad issue of reaching out to tell the person the dream which made me sound crazy, right? Especially when the person denies that the dream is even true. I have so many questions and what ifs. *Lord, what is this gift you have given me?*

Lessons Learned

How many of us are still hurt from something that happened to us as children? We are unforgiving. We are mad. We are sad. These emotions are normal due to those circumstances, yet God wants us to have self-control. He wants us to react in a godly way, having the fruit of the Spirit: love, joy, peace, patience, kindness, goodness, faithfulness, gentleness and self-control (Galatians 5:22 NLT). It doesn't say "fruits," it says "fruit" because although many are named, they are all one.

The fruit of the Spirit is the power of God that enables us to become Christ-like. These are all attributes that God expects us to develop though we are disobedient to God. We mock Him, are rebellious and reject Him; yet, God continues to see us as He made us to be and not as our mistakes. Look at the fruit. Look at someone doing you wrong and hurting you. More than likely, exercising the fruit of the Spirit isn't your first reaction or response. It would likely be the total opposite. God teaches us a better way to do it. It is hard, but nothing is too hard with Christ.

Chapter Two:
Siblings

I don't think my sister likes me. She loves me, but doesn't care for me. One day, I wanted to go somewhere with my sister and she told me, "No." I started following her anyway. It was freezing outside, and I continued to follow her. We argued. She took the Clear Fruit drink that was in her hand and threw it in my face on that frigid winter day. I felt like I had drowned. As the juice crystallized on my hair and face, I stood there in the middle of the sidewalk furious.

"Take your butt home! Stop following me," she hollered. I wondered if she hated me. Why did we always fight?

I was thirteen or fourteen around the time I received my $2500 inheritance from Grandma Jappie. My mom had to get us state I.D.s to cash the checks, which were in our names. I knew I wasn't given the whole $2500. My mom gave me $1000 and told me to not buy anyone else *nothing*.

I had a friend I would hang with and spend the night over her house. I ate there and her parents treated me like their own. I took her shopping with me and didn't tell my mom that I spent a part of my inheritance on my friend. One day, this same friend wanted to fight me about a week after we went shopping. She accused me of losing a piece of her daddy's game. I was so confused because I did not touch her dad's game. In fact, I offered to give her money for the game and she took it.

One day after taking the money, she walked down the street with her sister, coming to fight me. She said I was talking about her. I did not want to fight this girl because I considered her to be my friend. I had love for her. She hit me, pushed me and pulled my hair, but I still refused to fight her. I just cried.

My mama and sister got mad because I wouldn't fight my *friend*. This friend then yelled out, "That's why I took your money. Nah!" When my mom heard that, not only did she beat me but so did my sister. Everyone laughed because I got beat up by three people. My mom said, "I been tired of you." That phrase says a lot.

I was told I talked too much. I had a smart mouth. My mouth was extremely *smart*. I always had something to say and always had to have the last word. As a little girl, I was very quiet and soft spoken. I was always told to speak up, and to open my mouth if I had something to say. I just could not speak any louder and didn't know how to. As a result, I got whipped for it. I was told if I don't open my mouth to be heard, I would get my butt beat. I finally began to open my mouth loudly. Yet, my words always came out as if I was yelling. I had to yell in order to be heard. When yelling, I could never yell and sound sweet. When I yelled, it always came out harsh.

My sister and I have children by two brothers. Her children's father used to date my friend when we were sixteen. I never cared for him because of his character. Later down the years, I connected with my third son's dad through his female cousin. My sister started to come around, so she hooked up with his brother, the one my friend had dated. I never liked him because he was whorish. He would say inappropriate stuff to me and touch me in sneaky ways. My sister saw it but couldn't say anything because they were not together at the time. He began to flirt with her and they hooked up. Well, after that, she looked at me funny. He had told his friends that I looked better than my sister, but her body was better than mine. *Why was I even in your conversation?* It seemed that since we both dated brothers, they were comparing who was the better catch. After some years, my relationship ended due to domestic violence, but my sister was still in her relationship.

I started talking to Stanley, who was their close childhood friend. One day while at my sister's house, Stanley and I snuck in the basement to have sex. I was suspicious about what was about to happen. It seemed that these guys wanted to do what was something called the "switch-a-roo." They had sex with young ladies in the dark, then excused themselves to switch positions and/or people altogether. I wasn't having it. I don't know why they even tried. When Stanley got up, I got up, too.

"What you doing?" Stanley asked.

"Putting my clothes on." Then, my sister instantly called downstairs.

"Doug, Doug?"

No response.

"It's only me and Stanley down here," I responded. My sister flicked the light on and to my surprise, this dude was standing against the wall by a closet. I went off.

"Why is he down here?" I asked. I went off on Stanley, asking did he know he was down there. My sister went off and told me that I wasn't welcome back at her house. I have no idea why she didn't believe that I had no idea he was in the basement with us. I believe after all these years, she carries that.

Before that all happened, we all were living together in one house when we were both with the two brothers. There was ten or more people living in that house. It was like a squatter house. Slowly but surely, everyone began to move out because the house had been purchased, so we had to move. My sister got her a house, but it took me a while longer.

I had lost my job from always going to work bruised and my son's abusive father causing a scene. When he finally got locked up, I had to start over. I remained in the house and talked to the landlord about paying something to stay there. I made arrangements to pay, but then the gas got cut off. It was the winter and freezing. I asked my sister could I move in with her until I got on my feet. She told me flat out no, saying she had no room for us. We could have slept on the floor. I just needed my boys safe and warm. Yet she refused. So, I rolled up my sleeves and begin to do what I had to do.

I looked for work and went to several places to get clothing. On the bus ride home, I saw a childhood friend and he carried my bags for me. We were cool, so I wasn't embarrassed or anything. We talked, I thanked him and gave him my number. One day, he called me and wanted to talk to me. After a while, we began dating. After being intimate a few times, he decided he no longer wanted me living in that house. He talked to his mama and asked if I could stay with them for a few weeks. Lawrence was two years younger than me. His mom and I knew each other, and she was aware of my past. Here I am with three children, and her son asked if we could stay there. She asked me about my intentions with her son.

"I liked him but didn't know where the relationship would go," I explained. "I have baggage that you don't approve of. I want nothing from your son but his heart." She said, "Okay."

This was the situation where my sister told me I couldn't move in with her. I started working at a place called Copy Corps making $10.00 an hour. This was such an awesome opportunity for me to get back on my feet. Some friends babysat my children and I paid them. By my first month, I saved up enough to rent my first home. Lawrence and I moved in together. His father and friends disliked it. I had three children and a horrible past, but he was in love. We argued many days because he was teased by his friends for being with "*loose* Mia." He was the highlight of their jokes.

He got into a fight with my brother because although he was with me, he also joined in the jokes about me. My brother ended up knocking his tooth out and he had to wear a crown. The fact that I *used* to be "loose" was a constant topic of our arguments, so as an adult, I couldn't be trusted. How can you explain to someone that you are not what you used to be? Changed behavior, right? Yet, when people are set in their ways and their mind is made up, there is nothing you can do.

My future ex-husband, Stanley was the childhood friend of my third son's father and he was already in a relationship. We reconnected, had sex in my sister's basement again and got pregnant with my fourth child. I knew it was not my boyfriend's baby, but I had to break the news to them both. I mean my boyfriend couldn't be mad because of what he did. I used to wonder why every month at a certain day we would never have sex. God had showed me in a dream him cheating and the girl gave him something. After being shown twice, I sat him down and told him the dream. He broke down crying saying that he was sorry. He prayed that he didn't infect me because he had herpes.

"The disease that is not curable?" I asked.

"Yes, I just didn't know how to tell you. That's why when I had an outbreak, I wouldn't have sex with you," he explained.

I was so hurt, yet glorifying God. *Lord, you kept me from getting this virus. I had been with this guy, unprotected, in all ways imaginable and you kept me.* I knew then the relationship was over. I just didn't how to end it. I did what I knew how to do and that was finding and putting my time into another man to get over that very dysfunctional one. He got a long-term disease, and I got a long-term child.

Stanley called me when he found out from my sister, and all he asked was, "Is it mine?" I said yes. He asked if I was keeping it? I said yes. He said you better not sleep with no one while you are carrying my baby. I said okay. The rest is history.

Sitting together is a must for me and my children. Unity. Talking. Honesty. We are open with each other. It's a desire and a prayer. Yet, on some days, it is hard to get the children to get along. Siblings! They are at the age where they are arguing a lot. Two of my boys, Zamar and Zaire, have a competitive spirit and oh my Lord, I dislike it. What bothers me is that as a child, I was talked about and was an outcast from my siblings. As a teen, I fought a lot with my sister. After I got pregnant, I stopped going places with her like I used to because I didn't like what she did.

Things took a turn as I got older. I started to see that I was the one who seemed to get neglected or ganged up on due to my humility. Each one of my mother's children had their share of issues which had a lot to do with our poor home situation. My sister gravitated to older men to get her needs met. My little brother seemed to gravitate toward the streets and gangs which caused him to go to juvenile at age sixteen. My baby brother had issues from a child that I never knew about until we got older. I found out our dad raped him as a toddler. Being raped by our junkie father at age four caused my brother pain for the rest of his life. People talked about him because he had an issue of not holding his bowels, coupled with being poor. People did not care to understand his situation, especially other children. I found days when I had to fight for my brother's peace or at least be his peace.

Lessons Learned

We are to love our enemies and pray for those who persecute us (Matthew 5:44 ESV). Living in the past will do nothing but keep you bound. How can we move forward by looking back? God said in His word, *No one who puts a hand to the plow and looks back is fit for the Kingdom of God* (Luke 9:62 ESV). I look at this verse as saying no one who is called to work should look back. God is a God of moving forward. He doesn't go back. He doesn't need to.

Jesus said, *It is finished (John 19:30 ESV)*. God says we are forgiven of our sins once we confess (1 John 1:9). Things we did. Things that are in the past. It's why God allows the Holy Spirit to show us the future, things to come, regarding His kingdom. What we endured in the past was just our cross that we had to carry for His glory. It happened; now, let God light shine through. You survived. You're overcoming through Christ. Tell your story so that many who are enduring can be faithful and move in faith with motivation by the example of your experience.

Chapter Three:

Fathers

I never had a loving relationship with my father, but I loved *him*. I was always the emotional type. I hugged and loved to be up under my parents. My dad was his father's only child; yet, he had siblings on his mother's side. I never really knew my dad's story as a child. No one talked about it. Something must have happened to push him into the drug life he led.

The day we moved out from our childhood home is when my mom told us that they were divorcing. My dad watched everyone walk out the door as we got in my aunt's car. I thought we left everything, but my mom just left it until we found a place. No one said goodbye to my dad except for me. I hugged him and told him I love him. He said, "You're the only one who does." My sister asked me why did I hug him. I asked, "Why didn't you?" That question was met with scolding looks.

Although my mom was very active in school and into sports, she was a 400-pound-woman. However, after we moved, my mom dramatically began to lose a lot of weight. I realized it was the stress and drugs. We moved in with my aunt and her friend who stayed upstairs in a two-family flat. My mom didn't stay. I can't recall where she went.

It was just me and my sister. I don't remember the boys being there. We were still in school, so my aunt took us and dropped us off back to her house. We were only there for about three weeks; however, those weeks are long when you're somewhere no one wants you to be. I can't get over the look of my aunt's friend's eyes whenever she looked at me. It was always a blank look. I would always be so happy to see her because she seemed fun and lively whenever she came over for the holidays or when I looked at the pictures of her. Personally, she didn't say much around me even when I spoke. One time I overheard her and my aunt discussing about how much longer until we left. Her landlord lived downstairs and complained about the noise. We were confined to one room and barely moved.

I was so happy to still attend the same school. We stayed up the street from the elementary school. I got to see my dad daily after school as we waited on my aunt. Unfortunately, some days my dad wasn't there. Most days, he was not as happy to see us. It was more like a "Hey y'all," then would say that he loved us; however, I believe he said it as a cliché.

My dad never came around us after that. When my paternal grandmother died, he didn't even go to her funeral. He couldn't be found. My grandmother left $2500 to each grandchild, and left my dad $100,000 and her house. A house he could have given to his children. I saw my dad only three times after he and my mom divorced:

1. When my paternal grandfather died.

2. When I called my dad in 2011 before I got married. My ex-husband wanted to ask my dad for my hand in marriage. My dad didn't come to the ceremony.

3. When I was at the Samaritan Center in Detroit. I was walking out the door when he was already walking away from the building. I recognized my dad's walk. I said, "Hey" as I walked toward him. He stopped and asked, "Can I help you ma'am?"

"Daddy, it's me," I said.

"Mia?"

"Yes."

"I'm sorry. I didn't know who you were." He and I exchanged phone numbers, but he rarely called or answered.

Five years ago, when I called my dad's lady friend, she told me that he was in rehab. She told me that he usually checks into the center every first of the month because he owes people money. He would hide out to not pay the money he owed, but what happened when he got out? I have been praying that he's okay. I miss him. I would love to know that he's alright.

My mom met a man named Aubrey who loved her and us. Aubrey and I had a special relationship. He always spoke inspiration into my life. He was a drunk and cursed a lot, but he was nice to me. Even after he and my mom broke up. As an adult, I continued to visit him until the day he died. He always said he loved my mom. My mom said he drank too much and liked to argue. Knowing the men my mom had coming and going, I know that was the root of many arguments.

My son's father, Arthur, went to jail when I was pregnant with our son on gun charges. He was so hung up on not going to jail that he told me to tell the judge it was my gun. The calls were recorded and he got sentenced for it. This man harassed me from jail. He called the house and ran up the bill. I was paying $75.00 monthly for transportation to Adrian, Michigan to see him. He would even call me at my job while working at Copy Corps. I was pulled into the manager's office and was told not to accept the calls; however, I was not the one accepting the calls. The nosey shift manager would accept them and then pass me the phone. I would hang up and he would call back to leave a message that he was going to kill me.

Sure enough, when he got out of jail, he came banging on the door and I refused to let him in. He kicked the door open and physically attacked me as I held our son. He didn't even care that I dropped our son during all this. As I picked our son up and cradled him, he continued punching me in my face like I was a boxer. He was a huge guy and I was small in frame, weighing about 165 pounds. I cannot remember what made him stop beating me. I do know his pants fell down and I grabbed his testicles as he punched me. He laughed.

My brother came over, saw the door open and blood everywhere. So, he called 911 and I was forced to press charges. I was scared due to their family history of violence. When the police came, they took the report and took a picture of my face. He came back extra drunk and he was arrested outside trying to run.

I used to let Arthur drive my car because he was "the man" in the house. When I was getting in the car on my way to court, his brother came and wanted to fight me over the car, saying it was his brother's car and started snatching wires out the car. As a result, I wasn't able to make it to court and had to catch the bus on the next court date.

I was living in a house that Arthur's family was squatting in from when their mom moved out years before. No one paid no rent or utilities, and everything was on illegally. In court, he told the judge I was in his house and wouldn't let him in so he kicked the door down. He claimed he did not know I was behind it with the baby, but that's how my eye got damaged.

In 2005, my third oldest son's father went to jail for domestic violence when he broke my nose. In 2018, I started letting my son visit him and even live with him because my son showed anger issues. He was very disrespectful and tried to wrestle with me, so he left to be with his dad. His dad is very abusive, even to his nieces and mother. I've prayed for my son, and I've prayed that generational curse of hitting women, alcoholism, and disrespect would not be my son's testimony.

My son was around the foolishness for two weeks. His dad got drunk and started acting a fool and beat his girlfriend with a car battery. He ended up going to jail and she pressed charges. It's sad that after many years, this man never learned his lesson on abusing women. Thank God for that woman pressing charges. Sad that she had to endure being beaten. I advise any woman that no matter how much you love a man, love yourself enough to know you are not to be hit on.

It's a certain point in life when we get this concept. Even as a parent, if you discipline your children by spanking them, it shouldn't be done in a way that causes physical damage. No one deserves to be beaten like they've been in a fight. You are not a punching bag. Are you a drum? You are not to be beaten on.

Lessons Learned

Looking back, I could have had reasons to complain about the hurt and pain. God loves me and has done so much that I choose to glorify Him. I feel sad going through at times knowing people are taking advantage of me, or when things are falling apart. I look at the character of God and His history of always being there. I stand faithful in trusting God to turn things around no matter how long I have to wait.

God has a way of answering your prayers where He gets you to change your answer. God doesn't talk for no reason, and no prayer is answered in part. God will answer you and give you the solution needed for change. Remember,

He knows our heart's desires. I prayed and asked, "Why is this happening?" God said because I need you to disconnect, let go, move on, tell somebody and get help. Break the generational curses of bondage that you have dealt with.

Chapter Four:

The Children

How can you explain your desire to have ten children without someone calling you crazy? It was a desire for me at age fourteen. I remember sitting on my porch and talking to my baby doll. I would kiss and hold my baby doll. A lady next door saw me and said, "You caring for that doll a little too much. You better not be thinking of having one." *No ma'am, not thinking of having one.* As she walked off, I told God I wanted ten. Such a strange thing to desire. I just wanted someone to love and for them to sincerely love me back. Was I selfish? I don't know.

I remember playing the Game of Life with my siblings and for some reason, I didn't look at it as a game. I actually thought it was my destiny every time we played, although the journey of the game is preplanned. No matter what I chose or how the wheel spun, I always ended up with the same results. Six boys and rich. You know, the car couldn't hold more than a certain number of pegs. My siblings would always laugh about how many children I had.

People questioned why I continued to have children and couldn't take care of them. If people only knew my story. I often had jobs. I have training in many areas. I have been to college. The issue was not being able to leave my children with just anyone. Too many money hungry individuals. I refuse to worry about my children's well-being while I worked. I did that before and I found out my children were hurt by the very ones I trusted to protect them.

People thought that because I had numerous children that I received cash government assistance. Yes, I received food stamps but nothing else. I heard stories of other women getting money for school clothing from the state, but I never did. When I got pregnant with my twins in 2006, I was receiving cash assistance at that time. I called my worker to tell her about my issue with my twins. I thought that people cared more than they really did. I called to tell her I had to deliver my babies early since I was carrying a stillborn. When my worker picked up the phone, I introduced myself and she instantly said, "Hold on." I heard her say, "She always having all these babies and calling begging." I was hurt. When she picked up the phone again, I politely stated, "You know you didn't put me on hold? I heard what you said." This was the same worker who called me every time it was time to get my cash assistance to sell me the resources I called her for like new furniture. She would always have something for me to buy from her.

Upon delivering the twins, the girl was stillborn and my son, Zamar, survived. He was able to receive SSI disability since he was born premature and needed extra care. He was hospitalized for a month and needed to weigh four pounds to come home. One week after being home, Zamar stopped breathing and I had to do CPR on him. He was so tiny and I was so afraid; yet, I pushed fear to the side to save him. I called 911 and they told me to do CPR while they were on their way. When they got there, Zamar was breathing. They asked me if I wanted to go to the hospital, and I said yes. The closest hospital was St. John on Moross; however, I needed to get Zamar to Children's Hospital where they specialized in premature babies. So, I had to find a way.

I went outside in the rain and my van's window was busted out on the side. Who could have done this? There is no telling who damaged the window. I had called Zamar's dad and dropped the other children off at my boyfriend's sister's house and headed to the hospital. It was a 20-minute ride. I did not know my son kept dying on the way there. I had to shake him to get a response.

We got to the ER, and my son was still slipping in and out of consciousness. In order to revive him, due to him being so small, they had to thump the bottom of his feet. It was so hard to watch them poke and shake my baby, who was unresponsive. I knew God took me deeper into faith and trust with Him. They had to shave my baby's head to start an IV since he was so little. They could not find any veins anywhere else.

My baby was swollen and I was so hurt. His father, who was faithless, as well as some doctors, decided to tell me to think of the possibility of him not making it. I told them I could not receive that, and that I brought him there because they are the best. I asked them to do their best.

My baby was in the hospital for three weeks. I barely had money to get to him, but I called daily. I went up to the hospital when I could. I did not have much support. I didn't have a church home at the time, so there was no pastor or anyone to call upon for prayer. However, I did have some holy anointing oil that was given to me by a lady at church.

One day, I went to the hospital with his dad. Whenever I visited Zamar, I would anoint his forehead and pray healing prayers over him that I got off the Internet. His dad told me not to put "that stuff" on his forehead. He said I was doing too much, praying out loud, and trying to act saved when I was not. I made a mental note to not bring him with me again. The more I prayed, the more faithful I became.

A week went by with no improvement in Zamar's health. He was still on a breathing machine and I continued to trust God. I checked in every shift with a phone call. Every nurse had to get a call from me. I needed to know when each doctor came and went.

I lacked support with my other four children. I had to pay someone to keep them to go see my baby. If I had no money to pay or gas, I could not go see him. That was the worst feeling for me. His dad was supposed to be there but, of course, he was not. All my son's life, this man questioned who his father was. I told him to get a blood test, but he refused.

On top of all I was going through with Zamar, someone went around saying that the twins were not his children. The girl twin was light-skinned like his other children; however, Zamar came out dark-skinned. Sadly, it was my brother who spread that rumor. Why at a time like this would my brother do that to me? I asked my brother what would give him the right to say those things. He said, "Be real; that is not his baby. He looks like Smooth. All of your other children are light skinned." I stated Zamar and David, who was five years old at the time, were both dark like me. Is that your proof that I supposedly cheated? I asked him, "What am I gaining from this?" I got a man I love, and yet he cheats on me and does not help me with *his* children. But you think I would force a child on him just to keep him? No. I would never do that.

So, I questioned my brother about Lawrence's murder. I asked him when did Lawrence die. He stated 2005. I confirmed my son was born February of 2007. How could my son be his child? I didn't sleep with him after we broke up because I found out he had herpes. Nevertheless, bringing closure to a ten-year lie started by my own brother was definitely a relief. I still wonder why would my brother do that.

There was a time when my cash assistance from the state had exhausted. I received a lump sum of benefits and guess who had first withdrawal for payments? The Department of Human Services (DHS), the State of Michigan. They received $3000 up front because I had received those benefits and cash assistance. They stated that any funds that I received was a loan. I didn't know that. When we were homeless and I didn't have any income, I asked if I could apply for assistance since they took the money back. They told me no. There was no help other than what God sent. I received no government assistance, but I did receive assistance from American Red Cross. Everything I was blessed with came from friends, family and even Facebook friends.

I was not ashamed about what we wore. It was other people's taste, but we were provided for. I felt it was easier for people to go in their closet than to go in their pockets. I asked no one for money. My concern was clothing, my children and putting a roof over their heads. I trusted God to do the rest.

With my last daughter, I wore a scarf everywhere. We had just experienced the house fire and lost everything. We were given clothing, but nothing I was given could fit me. Most of the clothing I was given was dressy, and I did not feel like dressing up. I was so miserable. My ex-husband denied the baby. I was so depressed. I called on my children to do mostly everything, but fussed at them when they didn't do things right.

When I was a teenager, I used to steal to provide for my oldest son. Before I became employed at 16, I had a situation where I decided to steal a pack of diapers for my oldest son. Although I got away with it, potential consequences from planting that seed of theft always haunted me. As I grew in Christ and in the knowledge of His Word, I understood that you'll reap what you sow (Galatians 6:7). The lessons came around so that I could learn never to do it again.

When I was in my 20s, I received my income tax refund. I was with my third oldest son's dad. I got $5,000 back in my tax refund, and I went to the mall to get my son's dad some real diamond earrings. I stopped at my friend house and she walked me home. As we walked, a guy I knew from the block walked up to us and said, "Y'all gonna either give up sex or everything you got in your pockets." Since I knew him, I laughed, thinking he was playing.

"Oh, you think I'm joking?" He asked, as he pulled out a gun and pointed it at me. "Run y'all pockets."

My friend said she didn't have anything. I had all my money from cashing the refund check, so I gave him the money. He patted me down and got the diamond earrings, too. He said, "Now b**** run! Hurry up. If you tell anyone, I will kill you!"

We got to the house and I told my son's dad what happened. He beat me for being stupid enough to give him the money. The way he said it was like he would have preferred me getting raped as opposed to giving the guy the money. One day, we were at a gathering across the street from my house when the guy who robbed me showed up. I told my son's father that he was the one who robbed me. The guy denied it and I got beat for "lying," and for making him check a man and accusing him of something he "didn't do." The following week, the guy ended up getting killed. It was very sad. My heart was heavy because it seemed that he tried to rob another and lost his life. We must learn from the situations in our lives. God says if we live by the sword, we die by the sword (Matthew 26:52 KJV).

I have always had an issue with explaining myself since I was often misunderstood. Over time, I realized that people did not want to understand me. I never wrapped my mind around that. We are different and do not all think alike. There were people calling me crazy, me thinking I was crazy, and I felt I needed help. Things got so bad I used to have thoughts of checking myself into a mental institution. I called around to see how I could check in and how long I will have to stay in the facility. I wanted immediate results. I wanted the voices to shut up. I wanted to be able to sleep without being tormented. I wanted to understand why I did what I did and said what I said. I wanted to receive love like I loved others.

I was told to talk to a therapist, but I never knew which one. I was tired of reaching out for help, then getting hurt due to my vulnerability and being taken advantage of. I opened up and it was used to hurt me. I was not wise enough to discern who was real or not, who took their jobs seriously and who didn't. I didn't know you could reach out to professionals and people with titles for help only for them to turn you away or only half help you.

There was a time when my second oldest son took me through hell. He joined a gang, fought me and was stealing. It was too much. He would even smoke weed out of my baby's breathing machine for asthma. Three days before the house fire, he got my house shot up because he wanted to "gang bang."

In fact, my second oldest kept running away, back to the streets. One day, I found him sleeping in our old burned-out house. He made a fort under the table with blankets to keep the smell out, according to him. I continued to call the police on Javonte. They boarded up the house. My red Durango was still there in the driveway until I got it moved. My son began to sleep in the truck and light fire to keep warm. I called to get it impounded for $125. I had no choice. He was sixteen and I needed him home and safe. Yet, having him at home caused so much friction.

My son ended up at a house party when the police approached him. He decided to fight with the officer, was arrested, then sent back to me on a tether. However, he didn't abide by the rules and ended up in juvenile. He stayed there from age sixteen to eighteen. Being in juvenile saved his life.

My son received the help he needed — schooling, counseling and medication. While he was there, he was diagnosed with schizophrenia.

I found out that he had been mistreated as a child by his brother's family. He told me that he doesn't blame me. He said I wasn't there to know and he never told me. No one would lie about that. I got upset because I didn't understand why he wouldn't say anything. Who did it? I did not let this go unquestioned. I asked and, of course, these grown men denied anything; nevertheless, the truth will always be revealed.

My son was tormented and I never knew why. I wondered why he was always so angry, but I could never pinpoint the reason. I questioned if I was wrong in disciplining him. Did I love enough? Supply enough? Or protect enough? I missed the mark. He slipped through my fingers and I can't do anything to change it. He was so mad at me about people mistreating him that I knew nothing about at the time. He cursed me out at times. I tried putting my emotions to the side so I could see what the issue really was. It can be so hard at times.

Even as I am writing, I am in tears. God always makes sure He provides for me and my children. I am in awe at how quickly He answers my prayers and how His Spirit dwells in His people to be there for me. I feel so undeserving at times, yet God tells me He will provide for me and He does just that.

How Did My Children Feel?

I asked my children to write me a page on their feelings. I could never tell what they were thinking although I was paying attention to them. I know my older children's behavior changed. There was more disrespect coming from my son Javonte, who was sixteen at the time. My son Darryll was thirteen years old and Zachary was ten. Both were acting up in school. I was told they were being bullied about their clothes and shoes. This stressed me out more because we lost everything and what we were wearing was gently used.

Javonte decided to join a gang. Out of order! I don't know if he was trying to fit in with his peers, but he was out robbing people and fighting. One day, I found bullets, a bunch of credit cards and an I.D. I called the police because I didn't want him around, bringing harm to us and others. I believe that when a child no longer respects their parents and is a threat to society, they need to be rehabilitated by professionals. My son got arrested and put on a tether.

God showed me in a dream that he got shot up, so I prayed and told the court to send him to juvenile. The judge was so against what I was saying. Yet, when my son began to go against their rules and became irate in court, they saw then that he needed some help. He was arrested first for fighting police officers. Young black men were known to get killed by police officers doing this. God spared my son life in spite of his ignorance.

My seven youngest children are really neutral in their emotions. They just knew we had a fire and that we had to move. The youngest children from David, age two; Malia, age one and Sylvia, four months don't remember. Shalea wasn't born yet. I'm glad God continues to cover them and their emotions from any recurring thoughts of the fire.

My oldest son, Dequan was eighteen at the time. He turned eighteen on July 3, 2016, and planned to ship right out to the Army. I didn't want him to go for personal reasons. I didn't want to lose him to an act of war violence, yet I couldn't stop him. He kept in touch and is doing well. He is married with two children.

Celebrating my third son's 18th birthday gave me a chance to praise God for his life. After giving birth to my son, I was checked vaginally and was told I had cervical cancer. I was told I had mild signs before, but it wouldn't affect the birth of my son. Many tests were performed throughout the pregnancy on what the cells looked like. Up until I gave birth, it was all about what the cells looked like. It wasn't harmful, and I didn't have to have fear giving birth. But after giving birth, I was told it was cervical cancer and I needed surgery. I had to wait six weeks after having my son to have the surgery, which is called a colposcopy. I was nineteen with three babies, dealing with cancer.

I had so many questions. I was scared. I was told that my possibilities of having more children were slim. They hoped the cells did not become aggressive by the time of my surgery. Gratefully, the surgery was a one-day procedure. I was able to get the cells lasered out and go home. It took me weeks to heal inside. My mental state was all over the place. I just had a baby by a man who abused me and he was in jail for carrying a gun and served a two-year sentence.

I dealt with his family thinking I caught a disease from someone. They didn't understand how one could get cancer in their vagina. They said it was from me sleeping around, which had me thinking about being promiscuous in my teen years. *Was this my punishment for being with different men? God does not punish you and then heal you. Diseases are things of the world.*

Talking on the phone with my mom, she asked if I had cancer. I explained it was during my pregnancy with Darryll. I got emotional telling her my story because I was no longer going through it. She was there, but doesn't remember. She kept my two oldest boys, who were three and four years old. She asked how I got cancer and I didn't know. She told me how my grandmother had died from bone marrow cancer. I remember just praying hard to not have the cancer spread.

I told those around me at the time; yet, no one encouraged me much. I was in this walk alone spiritually. It was only me and God. I had to deal with all the thoughts of "what ifs." Dealing with not understanding. *How would I maintain a healthy lifestyle where I would not get this disease? What about going into remission? Would I have children ever again?* I was in such a depressed state and struggling with three children. We lived in an almost vacant house that was damaged with no gas, and the lights were on illegally. I had to do something.

As parents, when we go through certain issues, we don't think about our children and their feelings. How do you teach when you are going through yourself? Many days, I have pushed my emotions aside to deal with my children. It kept me distracted, yet I never received full, complete healing. I never let go fully because I never gave myself time to. How could I balance life for myself and my children?

The divorce affected them since I kept them from their dad because of many reasons that were appropriate to me. I hated that he saw us struggling and still would not help. I hated how he cheated on me. I hated how he denied my children. He told me he didn't want them, and he straight denied our last daughter altogether. It was so bad; he looked at her and would say, "Ugh, you look like your momma." When I was receiving food stamps, he would come over and just go in the refrigerator. I would fuss about it and yet, his response was those were his children's food stamps. If I could eat, so could he. So much mental abuse.

I had such low self-esteem. He shamed my body and I didn't want him around. I loved him, but hated how he treated me. Nevertheless, I continued to be with him sexually due to my natural urges that I did not know how to control. I felt dumb for loving a man who did not love me on the level I wanted to be loved. I hated how he got to go on with his life while I had to be the mother while trying to do fatherly things. I hated how he always claimed to want to see his children, and I hated that was all he did was *see* them. I hated how he used my struggles to talk about my parenting skills.

Starting from scratch, we were given used clothing. The children were given school clothing. I couldn't afford laundry detergent, so I washed their clothes two times a week. One day, he went to their school. This particular day, one of the girls wasted some sauce on herself and he talked about me so bad. I told him to buy me what was needed to keep their clothes clean. It was the least he could do. As it turned out, the court ordered him to pay $1600 a month.

The man is very skilled in roofing and home improvement; however, I am still living in a house with holes in the walls that needs painting and so much other work — all the things he could repair to at least keep his children safe.

My second oldest son was troublesome as a teen. He was the one God told me to put in juvenile due to the death threats upon his life. He used to steal, got into fights and got himself wrapped up in the wrong crowd of people. He tried to make a name for himself because he was a good fighter. He used that to make a reputation for himself in the streets. He always said he wanted to be a boxer. I explained to him that boxing is more than being able to punch someone hard. You had to be taught how to move, to listen, to be disciplined and to have stamina.

Well, my son got shot in his leg in June 2019 because he decided to destroy one of his associates' property. Along with that, he also posted some things on Facebook about the guy. As a result, the guy shot him in his leg to keep him from destroying more of his property. Through it all, God was with my son. My son was supposed to go to court to press charges. The officer wanted to help my son with resources such as housing, obtaining proper identification and completing school. My son was living from place to place. He had not lived with me since he was sixteen. He was extremely disrespectful to me. He cursed me out and was not a good example to his siblings. I allowed him stay at my house for one week so he could be somewhere safe while the detective assigned to the case tried to help him. Yet, my son continued to be disrespectful, so I said he couldn't stay.

One day, as I was doing my daughters' hair, my five oldest children had left with their mentor. As I finished with each girl's hair, they would go upstairs to play the game. Now, my front door was locked. When they returned home, Darryll, my 17-year old, asked, "Momma, have you seen my video game?"

"It's upstairs," I told him. "Where else would it be?"

"No, it's not," he replied with tears in his eyes. He said Javonte is outside and the little ones said Javonte came upstairs and told them to hush. This disturbed me that he could come in my house without my knowledge and take something from his brother.

I went outside to ask him about Darryll's video game, and Javonte took off on a bike. Darryll must have asked around if Javonte was trying to sell them a PlayStation 4. Many people inboxed me, saying they saw him and that he had sold the game. Darryll's game I.D. was registered to his email, so he knew when the person signed into the game. Darryll had to change his passcodes. Javonte would come around to use my Wi-Fi, but I also changed that passcode because I didn't want him around with that mentality. I could no longer deal with him breaking in my house, stealing, cursing me out and making my children uncomfortable.

One time, Darryll stole the tithe money out the lock box. A few months after the house fire in 2016, Darryll got a summer job working at our church. We were struggling at that time and Darryll had picked up a thievery spirit. Our church administrator called me, saying that Darryll was caught on camera tilting the lock box into the garbage bag.

She asked me did he have any money. I said no yet he may have spent it before getting home; I was not sure. Darryll denied it. My leaders talked with me and no one was sure if any money was even in the box; yet, the very situation was hard for me.

I had questions of why he would attempt to steal from the church. What did he need that he felt he couldn't ask for? I was so disturbed that I contemplated leaving the church. I was just that stressed. I didn't want to face anyone. I didn't think I could handle the talks about the situation. I didn't want anyone talking down about my son. He needed help, and that's what I prayed he got.

So, I reached out to the church administrator and asked her to keep it between us as we worked on getting my son some help. She agreed she would not include anyone. From that day forward, I watched her cultivate not only Darryll, but my son Zachary. She ministered to them, taught them what she knew about the media, sound room, and working the church's camera. She even paid them for their labor. Her labor of love showed them they didn't need to take anything. They must work hard for everything they do. With hard work comes rewards in due time. I thank her and my leaders for covering my son in love. They did give him a much-needed word and tough love. At the end of the lesson, I'm watching my son be a giver rather than a taker, glory to God. It taught me to stand up and face issues head on and not run from situations that arise.

My three oldest boys' fathers were not in their lives. After finding out that I was pregnant, my oldest son's father periodically slept with me because I was young—only sixteen. It was a thrill while I was pregnant. Yet knowing my background of poverty and my mother's lifestyle, he didn't receive me or my son. After I had my son, his dad came to get him one day when I was at school. I came home and my son was gone. I said, "Okay, great; his dad has him." I called him to see when he was bringing him home; he got to telling me that he is keeping my son permanently, that he was in Ohio and not planning to come back.

He felt like our son was living in a messed-up environment and I couldn't take care of him. My heart dropped. I was doing my best with my situation. I asked him why he couldn't talk to me about helping me instead of just snatching my son. It was a month-long battle. I prayed as humbly as I knew how to God, although I didn't know Him well. I knew of Him, and I knew that God saves and protects.

I knew He is all powerful. I had a simple prayer: *Please bring my baby home*. That's all I prayed daily, and God heard me.

I called the Ohio police and everyone would say, "That is his dad. If he signed the birth certificate, then you have no case." I did not understand much. I just went off what people said. God moved on my behalf. The man didn't have his life together and the person he was with confirmed life with a child in his situation wasn't easy. The man lived the street life and got locked up. The very struggle he talked about with me was his same struggle of living in poverty; yet, he made bad decisions to make ends meet while I worked and went to school. I got my son back and since then, I stayed away from him.

I lived my life as best as I could. When my son was seventeen, I stood at my church entrance as a greeter since I did not have my children with me this particular day. I saw this man frantically asking around about someone. He looked familiar. I heard him explaining to one of the greeters he been searching for this woman who had his son and had not seen her in seventeen years. Someone told him I go to this church. He was pronouncing my name as "Mya." The greeter was not familiar with my name, just my face. You know how it's easier to recognize faces before remembering one's name? So I walked up to him.

"Michael?"

"Mia?" He asked in confirmation.

"Yes."

"Where is my son?" He asked. He was frantically in need of seeing him. "Woman, where have you been hiding? I been looking for you for years. I gave him my phone number and address and he met his son. Our son, who was rebellious at that time, ended up living with his dad in Ohio. He stayed only for a season because the same behavior I dealt with, his dad refused to deal with. It was a lesson to my son that everyone has rules. I am not crazy or being mean; I'm teaching life lessons.

My son came back home, then the house fire occurred in 2015. He was graduating that June. Glory to God, someone purchased his prom tuxedo. The following July, my son joined the army. It was hard to let him go; he knew my feelings about the army. I prayed and trusted God to keep him. After serving, my son was discharged from the army right when Trump was elected. I was happy. He was discharged because he picked up too much weight.

After getting married, he said the income was not enough anyway to support him and his wife. He moved to Washington state with his wife's family. I have two grandchildren—a boy and a baby girl. My son is doing well, and I gave him some hard-earned wisdom about budgeting and shopping within their means.

Birthdays are hard. I'm currently fighting through the desire to call my ex-husband regarding our daughter's birthday. I used to let things go unsaid or honestly give him the benefit of the doubt of having sixteen children, so he may not remember all their birthdays. This was a lie I had planted in my own mind. I have eleven children and I remember all of their birthdays, including the birthdays of my friends and close family.

It really bothers me that this may be exactly one of the reasons why God said *not* to marry him. I married him anyway and eight children were born to our union. I believe I must deal with the absence. It affects my children and I am mainly in my emotions because I chose him in spite of what God said. I fell in love with someone who was not the best for me or my children. As I think of calling him, I ask myself *why*? What part of me will be soothed upon calling him? My daughter nor our other children are thinking of him, nor have they asked about their dad. I'm the one thinking about their dad being absent on our daughter's special day.

Instead of focusing on what is not being done, I will focus on what *is* being done. Life goes on. I will be what all my children need in this moment. I have no time to dwell on the "what nots." We can't survive off "what nots." I must move forward on the "what can's" — what can I do to make things better? What can I do to be what my children need in this moment? I trust God to send us what we need, whether we need the love of people or the hand of blessings from people. I trust God to provide for us. Where God guides, He provides.

As much as I've tried not to be frustrated or acknowledge the fact that my ex-husband did not contact our daughter on her birthday, a situation arose where I spoke to him anyway. He called my 18-year-old son's phone because I took our 15-year-old son's phone away due to misbehavior. He wanted me to give Zachary his phone to put an extension on it because his phone was connected with his other sisters on his dad's side. Our four daughters heard his voice and started screaming, "Hey daddy!" He was like, "Hey."

Malia grabbed the phone excitedly. "Daddy, it's my birthday!"

"I know," he said. Then, silence. Malia looked at the phone with anticipating of hearing more, but there was nothing. I furiously snatched the phone and questioned him.

"So, you know it's her birthday?"

"Yeah."

"So you can't tell her Happy Birthday? You couldn't call her?"

"I was going to wait until I get her something." At the point, I hurriedly got off the phone. What seemed like logic to him made no sense to me. Nevertheless, after seeing Malia's face and then watching her continue on with her birthday is what calmed me down.

Was I making a big deal out of nothing? I don't think so. I'm glad my baby didn't seem hurt; yet, I refused to ask how she felt. I didn't want her to feel bad about it, especially if she blew it off already. Knowing my feelings as a child regarding things like this and how I suppressed the hurt, it troubled my mind. My mind started to wander. I know my children are not me; but, what if they are like me and they are bothered by things like that? I must pray and be able and willing to minister to them in whatever area. In spite of our imperfections, I pray to minister to my children in ways it will be fruitful in their lives.

I cannot be afraid to talk about disappointments. That's an area I must grow in because I want to effectively minister to them and not belittle their dad. We are taught to never belittle a child's father to that child because it will make them resent you. I am praying to learn how to cover my children when they are hurt by their dad. I just pray to get it right. I believe in protecting my children as best as I can. It's just not fair to allow anyone—a brother, sister, dad, grandma, aunt or uncle—to do, say or treat them any kind of way.

God woke me up one day and my son, Darryll, was gone. I asked God which way to go and He told me what corner to turn at. Lo and behold, my son was on that corner, talking to some girl. I snatched him up and I sent her home. I watched her go home since she only stayed a few houses down. She began to walk slow like I didn't tell her to go home. I yelled, "Hurry up!" I do not know what he nor she thought.

I am trying my best to raise my children as God says in His Word, but it is not easy when you have disobedient children. I can say now that my son is eighteen and doing much better. He is more respectful and seem to be more focused. I do believe he is doing some things I do not approve of, like sneaking off to other places when he tells me he is at work. Yet, that will be revealed by God in His due time. Overall, my son turned out to be a mature, respectful young man. I pray for an obedient spirit.

I had an emotional day after taking my son, Zamar, to the doctor. I believe I never got closure over the fact that my son's twin sister was stillborn. Unknown to the nurse, she instructed me to bring the other twin in for her shots as well. However, she apologized upon learning that she was stillborn. When I heard that my son was still listed in the system as a twin, it was a hurtful, solemn reminder of his stillborn twin sister.

The clinic that treated me regularly said nothing about me continuously losing weight. I lost over thirty pounds with the twins. I was always sick and asked the doctor so many times what I needed to do. However, I was always told that I was fine. I asked if it was okay to lose weight while being pregnant with twins. They stated since I was already obese, it was okay. They always heard two heartbeats, and I was told my insurance only paid for so many visits.

At the end of January 2007, I went to the doctor ended up in the emergency room at the beginning of February 2007. I am certain it is in their system. Why did they not see that my baby was dying? Within the last seventeen days from when I checked into the ER, something mysteriously went wrong. I went to the ER again around February 18th due to a dark green discharge. My body was telling me something was wrong. My baby was gone and it was not my fault. I did not drink or smoke, and I tried to eat right. Someone dropped the ball. Information was not exchanged correctly. I wonder could this had been done differently or avoided, but I must be okay and at peace with the decision God made to come get His daughter. Thinking of the three babies I miscarried. Just thinking...Lord, comfort.

One time, I went to Saint Vincent De Paul and signed up for the LSP program for assistance with paying the utility bills. My caseworker told me to fill out paperwork at SER (state emergency request) for help. My worker would pay a portion and Saint Vincent De Paul would pay the remaining balance. At that time, I wasn't working and was in unpaid job training. I went to the class and received help for my bill; however, I was denied by the LSP program. I still needed to be on the program to budget out my income and to take care of my children. The representative I spoke to was harsh and asked why I called them.

"Didn't they pay $246 and your worker paid the rest?" said the representative.

"Yes, ma'am, they did," I responded. I tried to explain that my job training was unpaid. Meanwhile, she over-talked me and said that I am poor, based on the guidelines. The guideline is 20% and I was 2%. She questioned the fact that I made $80 a month. She did not let me explain that was the only income I made for that month upon switching to training for another job. Meanwhile, I allowed her to go on and talk to me like I was beneath her.

After asking if I understood, I began to explain that I wanted to update my income status with the pay rate and my first pay date. That's when her tone softened and told me that she, too, works from home. She began to compare everything I told her about my employment to hers. When I told her the future pay rate, she said, "Oh, you make more than me." When she asked my hours, I confirmed with her that I make my own schedule, so the hours may vary. Then, she told me she can make her own hours, which is why she called me. She said she called me the day before, but I didn't have a missed call or voicemail message. I gave her my info to verify if I could be approved, yet she used it as an opportunity to compare. I dislike how people with low income are treated.

Nevertheless, the day will come soon when I can pay every bill in full. *I pray now for increased finances to pay my bills without stress. Give me wisdom to invest and save so that if, God forbid, any emergencies arise, I won't have to take funds from a bill to supply a need. Lord, I thank You for the wisdom to manage my money and budget.*

My days are so full of being a mother, their teacher, the example, a cook, hairstylist, mediator and provider. I pray daily for balance, help, strength and rest. It is hard being what my children need at times. Most times, I fall short of the very thing they need. It is not easy to balance my life with my issues and struggles and having to make time for them all. Being pulled in nine directions; ten, if you include my 21-year-old son, Javonte, who needs my help and encouragement as he goes through his own healing process while he is in transitional housing to become independent.

My oldest son DeQuan is twenty-two, but does not come to me often with life issues. My heart hurts and yearns to be there for him and my two grandchildren, who I have never met in person. He lives so far away in Washington state, and I've never traveled by airplane. I only see them on Facebook or when their mom video calls me. I desire more of a relationship with them.

I dislike the struggle of needing so much while expecting help from the one who can't help. I understand providing care for children is a lot of work. My eight children by Stanley are lacking the father they so desire because he must spread himself in different ways. I am used to the behavior, which is sad; but I hold myself accountable for my decisions. I never make anyone do what I know they're supposed to do. I have no control over anyone.

My ex-husband has not complied with the court order to pay child support. If the court ordered child support and visitation and it hasn't been honored, then what can I do? I go about my life and take care of my children myself. My ex-husband periodically buys things for the children like shoes or gives them money. He will get two of the oldest boys' things they asked for. It was always a gift periodically that they asked for like a cell phone; however, it's never anything that they *need*.

I needed help managing their day-to-day living; nevertheless, I understood his struggle. I know all too well about financial hardship and being let down. His other children had a greater need and what my children needed was placed on hold. "Next time" would always be the answer. The "next time" was not from their natural father. God sent His vessels to minister to my children which ministered to me and blessed us all every time. God was showing us that He will provide and to not trust in man, but trust in Him. Man will let you down intentionally or unintentionally. Trust God to provide at all times.

We all have our good times and bad times; nevertheless, there is always someone worse off than you. There is always someone doing better than you. Don't forget to look at yourself as being better off than someone else. Don't focus on being someone less than. Encourage yourself in the Lord. Tests and trials come to make us strong and are used to build our character. Thank God for what He is doing in and through you and be a living testimony to those connected to you.

After losing the house from the fire, we were renting a place. I know the landlord didn't really want us at the house because I was constantly told about keeping up the property and about any damages I had to pay for. I understood all of that and agreed. I walked on eggshells around the house, afraid to touch anything or have my children touch anything. I kept everyone in one room so I could see everyone at all times. I walked through the house daily to make sure it was clean and not damaged.

I truly believe my behavior made my children feel like prisoners. I was intentionally imprisoning my children because of someone else. We were blessed with beds, furniture, and clothing. Nothing matched, but I can tell you that we were not on the floor. The thing with having used items is the wear and tear of it; therefore, having ten children would most likely cause those things to deteriorate quickly. Within a few months, we were back on the floor. I purchased furniture on an IOU. I had to pay $1200 when I got my income taxes for a dining room set, pictures, bed and couch, among other miscellaneous items. After a few weeks, I found out that the couch had bed bugs which spread throughout the other furniture. Always being the humble type and not wanting to hurt no one feelings, I decided not to pay the full amount.

After talking with God about desiring better, I wrote a letter to the church. As a result, we were blessed with a home. They decorated the entire house from top to bottom. On my dining room table, I had a photo frame that says, "Where God Guides, He Provides." Many people tend to plan what they desire to eat for the day or week. I planned to eat whatever was affordable at the moment. When I was not receiving government assistance (food stamps), I would get food boxes from church or other organizations that I call "mystery boxes." I used the items from those boxes and got creative with preparing our meals.

A few years ago when I lived in Warren, Michigan, there was a place called Hope Food Center. At Hope Food Center, people had to sign up to speak with a worker. They would ask questions about your household size and if you had any babies who needed diapers. I loved that they allowed you to shop for your own food. They gave out a card with how much weight of food you can get. The warehouse was set up like a grocery store. Bread and potatoes were not included with the weight of your food; those items were automatically given. You had a certain limit of items to get from each shelf. After you did your shopping, you would weigh your food and then grab your bread, potatoes and diapers, if needed. They also had a limit on miscellaneous items such as personal care items. I didn't feel embarrassed shopping at Hope Food Center; it actually made me feel independent.

Unfortunately, some places that are designed to help those in need make you feel like you are beneath them by talking down to you and treating you very poorly. No one should ever make you feel bad regardless of income status. I do understand that in customer service, there are times when you have to be stern with people you're serving. I strongly believe in treating everyone with kindness regardless of their income.

One time, I went to a place for assistance and a lady was so mean to me. Each answer she gave was with a bad attitude. However, I believe in communication.

"Are you okay?" I asked the lady.

"Why?" That's when I told her about how harsh she was being to me. I went on to tell her that I know she deals with so many people, and I understand that it can be rough depending on the moods of those she encounter. That's when she opened up and told me about some of the people she encountered daily, which led her to apologize to me. That's when I noticed how her demeanor changed and how compassionate she was with the next customer. I don't know how the rest of her day went, but sometimes we must look pass what we see and seek to identify the root of the action. I'm glad she even opened up to me, as it also helped me not to be offended myself.

Lessons Learned

I have made some bad decisions from reacting to things in life. I hit walls where I had to learn to make better decisions if I wanted better results. I am not ashamed of what I used to do or what I went through because if you look at me now, you can see the change God made in me. At the time, I didn't see it. I could not see it until God sat me down so I could see. I can only imagine what God was thinking. I praise and honor Him for His patience with me. His willingness to do a great work in me. For Him to see the God in me.

Chapter Five:

Overcoming

When the house fire first occurred, I glorified God for blessing us all to get out safely. So much gratefulness was in my heart, I had no room to focus on *not* having a home. God showed up immediately. The American Red Cross gave me $1800 for food, clothes and a hotel stay. For twelve people, that would only cover a few days at best. We went to a hotel that night and it was $200 a night for us so I decided the $1500 I had left would be to find a place to live.

I spent a few hundred on gas because we were sleeping on my sister's floor in Romulus. My transportation wasn't the best, so traveling an hour to Detroit and back was rough. I get emotional thinking about having to balance raising ten children at the time, along with the woes of a failing marriage, no assistance, along with us all sleeping on my sister's floor with no pillows. The bigger three boys slept in my niece's room, and my nieces slept together in one room. At the time, my baby was four months old. I had sciatic nerve damage in my legs and an umbilical hernia, so sleeping on the floor was an uncomfortable situation that I endured for almost two weeks.

I called the local news to see if help was available. I called shelters. I was discouraged when I called shelters and was informed that my family was too large. Even if they separated us, they still wouldn't have enough space. Can you imagine the scare of almost losing your family, along with going into a shelter that had to split up your family? That was *not* an option for me. I had to be with my children.

I called *Ruth to the Rescue,* a news segment on WDIV Channel Four. Although I was informed that I had a story, but my story wasn't "big enough." My case worker couldn't help either. I called the American Red Cross back to see if I could receive anything else. I was told that I received the maximum from them already. I called around to find a home to rent, but everyone wanted more money due to the large number of people, and the security deposit increased. I couldn't explain to them that although I have ten children, we would not tear their house up. I was so hurt, but kept a smile on my face for my children.

I still drove to Detroit to go to church. All I desired was for our basic needs to be met. I didn't want any cash. I saw a video of a dog who was homeless that received a home. I made a post on Facebook glorifying God, saying that if He made a way for a homeless dog, I trust Him to make a way for us, too. I got a comment from my church sister saying she had a rental property and to call her. God had His way.

I moved in this house in December 2016. It was given to me debt-free from the Detroit Rescue Mission and S.A.Y. Detroit which made national news. Grateful to receive an answered prayer. Not only that, but every appliance, furniture and knick-knack needed for every room was in the house upon us moving in. I didn't have to bring anything with us but our clothing. Walking through the house, we were all smiling. This was a place to call our own—a comfortable, clean home that was everything our heart desired—but the joy was short lived. Immediately, things started falling apart.

We flushed the toilet and feces came up in the drains and laundry sink in the basement. I had leaky pipes, and mice and bugs emerged. The house smelled really bad, and the roof leaked when it rained. When I turned the heat on, the paint on the walls started to peel. Some windows were still boarded up. I got the run around when I contacted the Detroit Rescue Mission regarding the home. I have many text messages from the day I moved in where I informed them that the house had some issues. I received many text messages, confirming they would get back to me. I reached out to everyone I thought of. Many people told me to call the *Hall of Shame*, another local news segment; yet, I refused to make the people out to be bad. I believed they would make it right. I wanted the home repaired properly. I didn't want any outside, negative attention.

I received a letter from a law firm regarding my house. The house that was provided to me and my family had a stack of violations. Yet, I never complained. I prayed and sought help to repair all that was broken. Things were repaired, but not correctly. Maybe the job was done according to what was paid.

The tickets stated "failure of owner to obtain certificate of compliance. Unlawful occupation of rental property without lead clearance; one or two family dwelling and failure to obtain certificate of registration for rental property," and the hearing was scheduled for December 19, 2018. However, I called about these issues in August 2018 and even went down to the City County Building during that time and was told that the issue would be resolved. Seemed like I was being sued by the City of Detroit or at least summoned to court for an issue I was not responsible for. How can you ticket the person you gave the house to on national television? How can you tell me I am unlawfully occupying the residence that was given to me? It all felt like a waste of time. Why was this happening?

The day I got the house, they sent the driver to pick us up due to transportation issues. The driver congratulated me and began to tell me his story. When he was done, he said, "I pray you keep the house."

"Why you say that?" I asked.

"They give away many houses and many people lose them. They give them back stating it's too much work."

"I don't see how you could give back a free house that they say is fully refurbished. If all I have to do is pay my bills and property taxes, then no problem." Little did I know that I would soon learn the reason why many of those people lost their homes.

It is very discouraging to know they raised one million dollars to work on and refurbish these homes, but it was only exterior work. Upon moving in, my home was painted incorrectly, and plug outlets were missing covers. One time, I posted a video of my children on Facebook, and my church sister said my outlets were dangerous. I told her that I was aware and was seeking help with getting it fixed.

I had lost my job shortly after the new year in 2017, due to calling off work to go to emergency with an umbilical hernia.

After lifting patients all day caused the hernia to protrude. It was very painful, so I was let go without any concern. I had to seek another form of employment that didn't require heavy lifting. I tried working at the post office, yet I had issues with the sciatic nerves in my left leg. So, walking was extremely painful at times. I was grateful my boys were of age where they could help out more.

After a year with no help, I called Legal Aid. The lawyer was looking into helping me until I told her I may possibly have to go to the news. She said she would not help me if I did that, and followed up by saying that she could not help me at all since I was the homeowner. Although I was not a homeowner at the time I sought help, I could not sue because I had no written contract to begin with. The whole thing was aired on national television. Although the world saw me get this house, it was not going to hold up in court. The lawyer did ask Detroit Rescue Mission for help with me getting the water deposit. They sent a check for $150 which I used to put on the deposit I needed to get my water turned on. I received a letter from the lawyer which stated she closed my case.

Being low income, I signed up for many resources that provided home repairs. I was denied since I did not have homeowner's insurance. In order to have homeowner's insurance, your home has to meet certain qualifications. My home was too damaged to insure based upon what I was told. If I insured the home, it would've been expensive since the home was already deteriorating. I was discouraged. God blessed me and led me here. I can't make a mockery of God and let people see that what He blessed me with someone took advantage.

I called one place to tell my story of how God blessed me. The guy said it didn't sound like a blessing to him, with all the issues. He said I needed to reconsider what it really is. I told him those who gave me the home were the issue, not God. It was a miracle and blessing from God to follow His instructions on receiving this home. Those people sold our story to receive a million dollars' worth of donations and were told that all the money went into the homes. I can't deny that they did put work into the home, yet it was not work done correctly and safely.

Talk about going from bad to worse. I went to the City of Detroit and found out that the property was on the demolition list. I was told the house failed an inspection. When I went to get the report of why it failed, the supervisor told me he doesn't have any record of any inspection. They usually keep that information, but he didn't know why there was no documentation on my property. He was very rude and nonchalant. I received many bills and tickets regarding noncompliance at the property as far as not having certification to live in the property after lead inspections.

I am praying for better. I promised God that I would be faithful in what is given. I trust God that where He guides, He will provide. In spite of the living conditions, God is providing. In spite of what is broken, crumbling, sinking, peeling or crawling around, God is still in the midst. He will fix and remodel it all. I am just praying the right people be led to do it. I trust Him to do it. Can't do anything but trust Him.

I thank God for days I could send my seventeen and fifteen-year-olds to the grocery store that is in walking distance. We learned to make everything stretch. My best friend would laugh and try to get me to stop stretching everything, but it became a habit. I water down every juice to make double of what we had. I would make one pack of hamburger stretch to feed us all. When I buy a family pack of chicken, I always cut the breasts or thighs in half.

Although raising my voice was required of me, I still got whipped or popped in my mouth for yelling or raising my voice. Of course, this cause confusion and I didn't know what to do with my voice. Either way it went — speaking softly or yelling, I got in trouble. As an adult, I yell. I raised my voice in my relationships and I got beat. I got beat for not answering a question, and I beat myself up when I yell at my children. I dislike being yelled at; yet, here I am doing something to my children that I didn't want done to me. I felt so neglectful. I just pray for balance and to learn how to watch my tone. Men told me to learn how to talk people. Thinking about it now, it took God to show me. I am still learning how to do this better. I am not ashamed to admit that I am now at a point where I am loving on everyone and being positive. I didn't want to offend anyone or hurt anyone's feelings. Was this healthy though? No one is positive all the time. Whenever I was upset, I held it all in, even when I was hurt, offended or frustrated. I hold it all in so I don't cause any problems. Suppressing it only created mind battles and anxiety attacks. In fact, I used to get bad headaches from holding issues in that I replayed in my mind.

The Impact of Molestation

When I was married, whenever my ex-husband used wake me up out my sleep to have sex, I always ended up fighting him. It got to the point he used to hit me back to wake me up. He told me continuously he was tired of having to fight me to have sex. The mental battles I fought stemmed from things I hadn't healed from. He even had sex with me while I slept with me only waking up for him to "finish".

I hated having sex with my husband because of the spirits I felt from him, along with knowing he had cheated. I took myself mentally to a numb state. He would be on top of me and would look into my eyes and ask what's wrong with me. I would be mummified. Many times, while being raped by my husband, he gave me a sexually transmitted disease. I thank God they were curable. I had trichomonas so many times, my doctor told me to stop sleeping with my own husband. He said my body is susceptible to AIDS because I had the virus so many times. He also stated that he can't continue to treat it. He gave me medication to give to my husband. It seemed like I was playing Russian Roulette with my life just to have someone. I told this man my secrets, my pain and my hurt. He had to treat me right...*right*? What would it take for me to realize that no matter what I did, I had made the wrong decision in marrying this man?

I had a dream years ago that my cousin (my uncle's son), his wife and baby were in the hospital. So, I reached out to his wife asking was everything okay, and she said yes. I had only met her once when he came to Detroit to visit. We didn't really communicate often. He was in the Army. When we talked periodically, it was about God and us missing each other. So when he came to visit, he had been married a while and had children. No daughter, just a son. When I finally found out they had a daughter, she was four. Years went by, and my cousin's wife called me and told me that my cousin was in jail. She explained that he had molested their daughter and would not stop. She said she gave him a chance to stop, yet he refused. She said he sought help and was changing. Then one day, they got into an argument and she called the police. When she mentioned the molestation, he was arrested and charged.

I ministered to her and shared how that the molestation spirit seed came from my uncle. I told her my story, and this woman turned on me. She blamed me for not telling her, told me that I needed counseling and that I should not be around any children until I got some. She said that as a woman of God, my discernment should have led me to warn her, and that I am at fault as much as he is. I told her that I am not my cousin. Yes, we come from the same family and experienced the same things, yet my mentality is trusting in God to keep me.

"Yeah, that's the same thing he said," she responded. He preached the word, but didn't live it. I just told her I am sad you are experiencing this. It is not my fault. I could have blamed her for knowing what he was doing to their daughter while giving him a chance to stop. I didn't because it was not the time to make her aware of her actions. She was hurting. She already was blaming me. All I could do was listen.

I prayed silently as I rejected all that she said about me. I had to know who I was in Christ. My situation would not define me like my cousin let it define him. I can't tell you why people do the very things that were done to them — on other people. I have a soft spot for people. Many people deal with hurt and behaviors differently. My cousin caused hurt with molestation, just like his father. My brother caused hurt with molestation, like my father molested him. I hurt myself by letting people take advantage of me.

I've always known that I'm not a dumb person and that I have a teachable spirit. I had a few friends who were controlling. I would have conversations where I would describe how to cook eggs my favorite way. Then I would learn how to make eggs their way. This friend told me I act like I'm dumb. She said I am a mind manipulator. Why would

I act like I didn't know how to make eggs just to learn someone else's way? I told her I never said I didn't know how to make eggs. I just wanted to learn a new way. This friend had many issues and yet, I endured the friendship for years. Nevertheless, it was emotionally draining. I found out that all my secrets and personal issues I shared with her, she shared with others and used to talk about me. It was only in finding a true friend in Hope that I began to understand how toxic my other "friendships" had been.

My Pending Divorce

Before we got married, he was not even allowed to come in the house since I was staying with a friend, so we had to meet outside. My friend's rule was that no man was allowed in her home since she was single. I lived with my friend from July to September 2011. I decided to purchase a house right across the street from her. I was approved for the house. I planned to get married three days after receiving the home. God showed me twice not to marry him. Nothing against Stanley, but God planned me to be someone else's wife. Yet, I wanted him.

I told Stanley I wanted a man of God. He had to be a constant church member. We had to go to marriage counseling and he had to be baptized. I had this list of demands for him to follow; however, I didn't realize that he could do all of that just to please me, and his heart still not be in it. I tried to pray daily with him, yet he would not open his mouth to pray or thank God. It was like pulling teeth and it turned into an argument, him accusing me of trying to make him do something. He would do it in God's time.

When I asked my ex-husband what he disliked about me, he said my mouth. I know I talk too much. I had a sharp tongue and refused to let a disagreement go. I confided in the wrong people many times. I didn't respect my ex-husband spiritually. I felt he was blind and would lead us into a ditch. I loved him in a worldly way and never looked at what he lacked spiritually. Then, I noticed that we both needed spiritual guidance. He was not willing to live the sanctified life. I depended on my knowledge and those in my church home to teach my ex-husband, yet I forgot that you have to be willing to learn.

We had a great relationship, yet having a lot of children may have been an inconvenience. I knew it was a lot. My children were a handful. I have one that will pee the bed, one who will poop on themselves, two that would steal food. It was a bit much, yet we endured.

How many women out here trying to make a man be something he is not? I used to get upset when he would say, "You're not my mother. Stop acting like it." I didn't realize how controlling I was trying to be. The more I sought God, the more I started to pull away from Stanley. I was focused, and then I got distracted again.

He started doing all that was on my list without me asking him. He came to church a month straight. We had marriage counseling where I sat and listened. I asked bishop one question: *What do you think I should do regarding marriage?* He said pray. Talk to God. I wanted him to give me a definitive yes or no whether I should get married. I believe bishop saw something and figured I would never be able to say he told me to do this or that when the marriage failed. He was sending me to God. God had already told me what to do and here I was, still being rebellious. I was doing everything right but with the wrong person. I was disobedient.

As Stanley prepared to get baptized, I knew then that I was making a mistake; however, I refused to turn. This man left church to go smoke a cigarette and they were looking for him. He was late for his own baptism. He put on the act to get the benefit of me. I was so gullible for him. I was paying his child support, doing everything I could to help him. He was not a bad person; he simply wasn't the husband for me.

Stanley was a male whore and drank a lot, and I disliked those things about him. We bumped heads constantly when I wanted to go to church because he said I went too much. There were things he disliked about the church people. If he was a man of God, those complaints would've been prayers interceded with me; yet he turned it into a reason to stay from the church. I felt horrible because I never wanted to be the one who makes a person run from church. To this day, he uses that information when he talks about me.

We must watch what we say at all times. Some things we must talk to God about. I was a babe in Christ, so this was a lesson to learn. A hard lesson, but God will be glorified. I married him and I knew the first night that I'd made a mistake; yet, I couldn't turn back. The night we got married, we did not have sex at all. He said we've been having sex already, so it's not important. He claimed all he wanted to do was to love me and take care of me.

He started working with one of the deacons at the church a week later. The job required him to be gone for weeks at a time and only come home on the weekend. I was not comfortable with that. I had just purchased the house; we didn't even have a toilet or water. I was going across the street to get water. I told him that I wasn't comfortable with this decision. He came back home and ever since then, he blamed me for him missing out on that job opportunity.

He started focusing his attention on video games, twenty-four hours a day. The man refused to touch me. I called a mother of the church and she gave me ideas. Join in on what he was doing. Dress sexy. I even made videos of myself and nothing worked. He actually critiqued the videos, which made me feel low. I thought of Eve's punishment for sin when God said that she would have a desire for her husband and he would have rule over her.

Three months after we got married, we were finally able to be intimate. Lo and behold, I got pregnant and all hell broke loose. He was so upset that he left me for seven months. I had a hard time accepting my baby that I was carrying. He was a seed from a unified marriage, or so I thought. The truth is my marriage was not unified. There was a back and forth battle in our marriage where we would fight and make up. I had four babies in the seven years we were married.

After many fights, I would put him out the house. He would get tired and couldn't deal with my attitude, but everything else as far as sex and my giving spirit, he took advantage of. He had no problems sleeping with me or me buying him whatever he wanted. For example, I took my whole income tax check in 2012 and paid $5000 worth of his traffic tickets. I kept the receipt book to remind me of how gullible I was until God had me to toss it in the garbage. I did that to help him get his driver's license, which he still doesn't have. My problem is I loved someone my Father forbid me to marry. Then, I had a problem of letting him go.

When God tells you to do something, it is always for your good. We must choose obedience, even when we do not understand. Finding out that my ex-husband slept with my mom was hard to deal with it. It caused trust issues in our relationship as a mother and a daughter. Sadly, I found out about the act before we got married, but I was already in love and had a child by him. I found out from his other children's mother and she used it to laugh at me. She said he told her how much he didn't love me and that was his proof. How desperate was I to be in love with a man who chose to be intimate with my mother? My mother continued to deny it before finally admitting that it happened before we got together. I wonder would that have made a difference in me being with him?

Whenever my mom came over, I watched my ex-husband like a hawk to make sure he was not doing or saying anything inappropriate with her. He acted like he disliked my mom. Despite what happened between them, I fought to make him respect her. Even in my insecurities, I tortured myself by living a life of bondage. I prayed constantly and I would always be shown visions of this man. God never left me in the dark about what this man was doing. Month by month, year by year, God had shown me the women he had been with. It got so bad that God even showed me my husband in my sister's bed. I woke up mad each time. I would ask him and I would ask her. They both denied it. I asked God what was it? Why was He showing me this? God said, "He will take this to his grave. Have I ever shown you anything just because? Know my character. I know it hurts, yet you have to trust Me and what I am showing you."

Many situations started to become questionable. I would put him out and he would go to my sister's house. I would call her and question why. She would say that is her brother. She knew him before we even got together. I noticed how they always went to the clubs and drink together after we got married. He would always tell me that she was sleeping with one of his friends, but who was *he* sleeping with? I noticed when my teen nieces would come over, they looked at him in a certain way as if they were used to seeing him. The more I saw, the more I got tired.

I tried three times to divorce him; yet, I believed it was my punishment for being disobedient the first time. The enemy didn't want me to be free. I was depressed, suicidal and homicidal. I was bitter. I turned to anyone who would listen. Friends were not friends — they were gossipers. They used my dumb decisions as a string to pull me along for their benefit. I fought constantly even while being pregnant to get this man's heart — to make him love me.

I went to church continuously and prayed daily. I knew God's word just was not living it. I thought I was. I wasn't sinning as far as drinking, smoking or committing adultery; yet, I was not trusting God wholeheartedly. I was not letting go when God said, "let go." I was told to let go or it would kill me. I wondered if it would be a natural death. Was I going to contract a virus? *Lord, you wouldn't let me die, would you?* Just as God told Adam and Eve to not eat from the tree of the knowledge of good and evil or they would surely die, in their disobedience, it caused separation from their Source. Their relationship with God was severed, which caused a spiritual disconnection.

Divorcing him was hard because of my emotions. I had a soul tie to my ex-husband. God said not to marry the man, so I had a hard time letting go. I used to think of all the possible reasons why my marriage did not work: *I had gotten fat. My attitude was not right. I did not keep myself up and I became unattractive to him. I was in church too much.* I told people our business. Although these reasons can be an issue in any marriage, the main reason my marriage did not work was because it was not supposed to.

Amos 3:3 KJV says, "Can two walk together, except they be agreed?" Second Corinthians 6:14 talks about not being unequally yoked. These are Scriptures that I did not live by. God gave me a personal word of *no*; yet, I was disobedient and prayed for a *yes*. God never said *yes*. He just threw His hands up. No matter what He showed me—the cheating, the abuse, the neglect, the usury, the dreams of my future—I always would pray against it. Pray for change. Trust God to do it. So unwise.

Yes, God shows us things to pray about, yet we must use wisdom and discernment. God is a God who wants faith and action. He shows you something. You respond appropriately to it. According to Brainly.com, reaction means, *an action performed or a feeling experienced in response to a situation or event.* Attributes of a reaction are anger, hurt, excitement, happiness, confusion, fear, sadness, denial, gratitude and acceptance. Then, you move on what you heard...appropriately. Action is doing something to achieve an aim or goal. Our reactions come from the action that was done first. Action: hit someone. Reaction: become angry. See?

He tells the story of me putting him out because he did not want to go to church. I remember putting him out, but not because he would not go to church. I was controlling and used God as a crutch. As for me and my house, we will serve the Lord. No one will live in my house and not serve God. This was a huge mistake I made. I could not make a grown man do anything, yet I definitely tried. I paid the bills and everything; so in my mind, since I do everything, do what I say. If you seek God and get a relationship with Him, you would know how to treat me and love me. I was so bitter. No matter what I did or said, it made my life worse and I was making his life miserable. If I was the only God that man saw, there is no wonder why he did not go to church. If he was disrespectful to me, that's exactly what he got in return.

This man used to steal money from me. After the house fire, we went our separate ways and that was an issue for me. Me and my children slept on my sister's floor and he went wherever. I didn't reach out to his family for help for various reasons, yet they were helpful anyway. A few gathered together to give me $100 each. My ex-husband went around telling them I had spent the money at the casino, which was a lie. His aunt told me personally she was giving me the money in my hands because of his character. When I found out what he told them, I sat him and his family down and talked with them. I told them that although I do go to the casino, the money I was given is to get a house with. I didn't tell my ex-husband because I was leaving him. After all, he left us when we had nothing.

The day the house caught fire, he went to have a drink. When he came back, we were outside as the house burned. He did not comfort me or my children. What hurt is his people were willing to take the electronics (big screen TV's, video games, etc.) to keep, yet me and my children had to wait until my sister arrived from Romulus to follow her home so we could be at her house.

I disliked the things I saw. It was like a disconnect when his family arrived versus mine. His family was concerned about him and mine was concerned about me and my children. From what I could see, he wasn't even concerned about the children. No one else offered anything other than my best friend. Yet I believed that in this situation, family had to step up.

I sat at the table with my ex-husband and gave every family member their money back. I thanked them and wrote a letter to the ones who were not there on the reason why I was giving the money back. I dislike anyone doing anything for me and throwing it in my face. Whenever anyone would do anything for me, I reimburse them back with more. People got used to that, especially my family. I would overpay and put myself in a hole. I knew what it felt like to have nothing, so I made sure I accommodated people for their time and money.

When I continued to deal with my ex-husband, I was disobeying what God told me to do. God said He would never leave me or forsake me; yet, how long did I think I could live a life opposite of what God said? As I was writing this book, my ex-husband called and we talked for over an hour about his feelings toward me. He thinks I am weird to want to meet his girlfriend, who he never said was his girlfriend. He says he is uncomfortable with talking about her to me. He doesn't want me to be with another man because he doesn't want me hurt. *The same person who hurt me is concerned about another man hurting me?* He says he don't even know if he will be with her for more than a year. He only living with her because he had issues at the place where he was staying. I felt he was bored and he knew I would give him good conversation.

My ex-husband came over to spend time with our children. For whatever reason, he didn't answer the phone when his pregnant girlfriend called. She decides to inbox me about dropping his clothes off and that I can have him back. I refused to respond. I looked in his phone to see that she was cursing, fussing and calling me all out my name. She threatened to send me videos of her twins, saying I will be mad after she hurt my feelings.

Being in the midst of their mess is not where I wanted to be. I assumed that he told her I lost one of our twins, which is why she thought telling me about her having his twins would hurt me. I am not mad that he has babies on the way. I have eight children by him that I get no help with. I pray for her and her heart. I do not want that man. Yes, he tries to sleep with me, but I no longer have a desire to be with him. Yes, I slept with him in the past due to me still loving him, but I no longer give in knowing I deserve better.

I pray for her and him. I pray he changes. I pray she sees her worth. You got him by cheating with him as the side woman while he was married. Now she believes she has a hold on him that will make him stay. She don't know the talks I have with him every time he approaches me. I question his motives. I pray he works on his relationship. I keep my distance even if it means him not seeing the children because I refuse to allow him to use the children to get to me.

She threatened in a text to bust out my windows and my window *mysteriously* got busted the next day, December 1, 2019, at 5:15 p.m. When I called him, he asked where I was? I stated that I was at home. He asked did I get into it with someone. *No. You know I don't go that route with drama.* I told him that his girl was the only one who threatened me. He told me he would call me back, but never did. I instantly and sincerely prayed for her. She definitely needs peace and healing.

I know *exactly* what she is going through. It is the reason I divorced him. I feel sorry for her heartache because she was a part of mine. I wouldn't wish that pain on anyone. It's not fair to be mistreated, and it is not fair to love and not receive true love in return. How could you give your all and get no more than half, if that, in return? Being pregnant by a man who could avoid you, reject you and cheat on you? You're the only one in a "situationship," settling for a man just to say you have one and yet, when he leaves, you wonder what he's doing. I refuse to be with someone who would continue to talk to the women he has on the side. My heart is too good to get stomped on and broken. My Abba Father has mended areas in my life and I refuse to let man intentionally pierce through to hurt and scar. It took a while to heal from my self-inflicted pain. I won't go back.

I never knew that a person of the opposite sex can make you feel ugly. To hear, "You think you cute, you just want attention," can damage one's self-esteem even more. Now, I make sure I know I'm cute and not to seek approval from anyone. God didn't create no mess, but after being divorced, I had to watch when I encountered my ex-husband. I'd catch him at times just staring at me. It bothers me when he approaches me sexually. I fell into sin through fornication with him after our divorce; however, there is no purpose to sleep with him continuously. I was his wife for seven years and he was not who God had for me.

I am more than my body. I am the same Mia I was when he married me, but I am wiser, more faithful and obedient to God. After fornicating with him, I would cry and avoid him. This man would message me asking, "When can we do it again?" I would go on to explain the relationship I wanted to have with God and how I hurt God every time I lay with him.

"So you can give it up whenever you want, but I can't have it when I want it?" That was his response, which showed me that he did not respect me. How could I argue when he was right? I would lay with him when I wanted to. He did not understand the spiritual battle I had by laying with him.

Gambling

How do you deal with life issues? Having a gambling addiction was to pacify not having enough money to make ends meet. Gambling temptations are not as strong as they used to be. I can refocus my attention and trust God to provide. The gambling spirit is so strong in the land. I would see people of God with titles in the lottery line or at the casino. Thanking God for allowing them to win. I was one of those people. You would definitely get a big debate regarding this. I used to think it wasn't hurting anyone, yet it hurts your trust relationship with God. That's the most important thing.

I pawned my laptop knowing I had to work and continue to write. *Am I trusting God with my whole heart? Am I glorifying you, Lord, like I should be?* When I said I was going to stop gambling, I would find myself at the casino. I was more concerned about solving the problems that needed to be solved with money. Each issue seemed different, but the root was the flesh—the lust of the eyes, the lust of the flesh, and the pride of life. I chose to focus on what I saw or felt.

Temptation is just a thought that comes to mind. We have a choice to act on it or not. If we know that we are not strong-willed, then we must call for help. God will answer. He will keep you until you are strong enough to say no. We need God to send us in another direction so we can refocus our attention.

Now, I choose to wait on God. I still do my part in seeking employment. I refuse to go back to gambling or asking their dad for help. In my mind, I believe there shouldn't be an issue of my children's father helping his children. Yet since I know the consequences of asking him for help, I choose not to. I would rather my Abba Father to send me the help I need without someone looking for favor in return.

The very man I committed the sin with had condemned me. I wasn't looked at or considered to be a Christian, righteous or a child of God, and it bothered me so much. But my God is a forgiver. I had an intimate conversation with my Heavenly Father. All I had to do was be honest with Him. I am able to handle my issues better now. When tempted, I can see the way God has given me to escape. I am learning and growing, and I give all glory to God. I'm unashamed.

The night before I filed for a divorce after three attempts, I laid on the couch, praying and worshipping. I was singing *Thirsty* by Marvin Sapp. Suddenly, I heard this rumbling in the spirit. At first, I thought it was my children upstairs, but I got quiet and I only heard it in my head. There was snarling and bumping. My heart began to beat extremely hard. I became afraid, but I heard, "keep worshipping." So, I got louder and louder, and then I heard, "Divorce. Let go." I said, "Lord, I don't have gas fare to get downtown."

"Do you trust me?" God asked. Thirty minutes later, I got a notification of $60 on my child support card — a card I hadn't received funds on in years. I received that sign.

I called my best friend that morning and no answer. I called others and no answer. I needed a push. I was nervous. I was emotional. I cried because I felt like a failure. I was in love with a man God said is not for me. How did I get here? How will I live past this? *What does my life hold now? I have eleven children — such a large bag. I know no one will want this life. I messed up bad, Lord! I went against you. Now, look at me.*

A friend called and encouraged me. As I turned in all the paperwork, standing at the desk, I listened to my pastor and first lady virtually on Facebook. I heard the pastor say, "Miss Branch?" I finished up and got to the car. God had them intercede in prayer for me. I wrote down the prayer. Every name of every person that interceded for me—almost 100 people prayed. It was that moment when I realized God would take care of me. He wants me to focus on Him, seeking first His Kingdom and His righteousness, and all else will be added.

As I look back on those prayers, I saw God grant the exact prayer requests. God continues to guide me while providing for us. We had not been in an extreme situation where I had to beg for anything. People just come from different directions blessing us. Although I am divorced, God stepped in to be the head of my life where He was supposed to be in the first place. God was putting His order back in my life. Glory to God.

Loneliness

After praying, I didn't realize how much doubt I had regarding my love life, or should I say my future. Will the love from the husband that God has for me be my portion? I deal with such double mindedness. I claim and believe God has a husband for me; yet, I doubt any man will accept me with all my children. At the drop of a hat, I will tell anyone how many children I have with gladness. I understand having that many children is rare. Usually, you hear of that number of children from those in the south or from the 1970s or earlier. People look at me and think I am younger or tell me I look great to have that many children. People will say they struggle with their few. I always tell them all glory belongs to God.

I have my struggles and my issues with my children, too; yet, God is always the source I go to when I need anything. Those closest to me know what I've dealt with. At times, I am transparent on social media. Nevertheless, I do it all to God's glory. Who can take some coal and make it a diamond? God can. He will and He wants to.

My Struggle with Masturbation

I've personally struggled with multiple addictions. When I relapsed with fornication, I was more concerned on the flesh being pleased. Lying in bed right after sinning, I asked the Lord what do I need to do? Why do I go months being obedient and then have these moments?

I heard "fast". Every time I fast, I have a battle with the enemy saying that I only want a fast to lose weight. I should have shut him down with the Word. I never fight as I should. My fast has not been food. Instead, I will not watch TV or talk on the telephone for that time. No, I am not feeding my flesh with worldly things, but my appetite for the world does not leave. I am not starving or depriving myself too long. My flesh is able to handle the three-day fast without food.

When people go to jail for doing something, they are mainly asked upon review if they are remorseful for the offense. What is their progress? The judge wants to know if they've been rehabilitated. Are they any longer a threat to the community? If their mindset has not changed, their chances of being free are slim to none. This is how I view my life as a child of God. God is trying to change me. He wants my life to be beneficial to the world. His Kingdom. We must die to the flesh daily.

Rehabilitation is the act of restoring someone to health or normal life through training and therapy after imprisonment, addiction, or illness; the action of restoring something that has been damaged to its formal condition; the action of restoring someone to formal privileges or reputation after a period of disfavor. Many of us need to be rehabilitated. Why is it so common for a person to run from the help? Many people would say, "I have to go to rehab," or they refuse to go to rehab. You have many who go through rehab after a relapse. Why do people dislike going to rehab centers?

Sometimes, we don't want to fight to pray. It becomes discouraging because we can cry out and yet don't feel God. Our feeling to satisfy the flesh is still there. We must understand with each breath we take that God is there. I cried often regarding sexual urges and desires. I felt like I was sinning by just having the urges. No, that was far from the truth. My urges were natural and were given to me from God with instructions! We are to unite with our spouse in marriage in order to fulfill these urges. Until then, we must pray for self-control.

We must have self-control, which is a fruit of the spirit. We don't want to abuse or misuse any part of our body by doing wrong. We relapse because we don't refocus. We must learn to focus our thinking. Watch what we allow to come through the channels of our eye and ear gates. We must be mindful of areas where temptation can enter. Include God in helping you refocus. He is the vital key to the transformation.

I am embarrassed because I thought I had been delivered from masturbation. Many don't talk much about the subject, and it is so needed. This is the act of sin as much as fornication. When I think of this, I think of God saying that people become "lovers of themselves" (2 Timothy 3:2). Yet, it is a concern for me that many seeds can sprout from this.

People are attracted to the same sex and marrying within their own gender. Odd isn't it; yet, what is the root? I always believed that I was not hurting anyone by masturbating. I was saving myself for marriage; yet, I was pleasing myself.

God created man for woman and for the act of marriage to be unified—not to please or be a lover of yourself. Man and woman shall be intimate together, and that is pleasing to God. In Genesis 4:1, it says nothing about Adam knowing himself or Eve knowing herself. Why am I writing this? It's because I'm struggling through my singleness after divorce. Coming from a place of being intimate whenever I wanted to, to not being able to. My body craves and yearns for what it was used to getting. That's why it was so easy to fall into fornication with my ex-husband. I was used to him. He was the only man my body was familiar with for fifteen years. God had to really hit me hard regarding this. The man is not my husband anymore. I cannot do things with him anymore.

I cannot be disobedient for a pleasurable moment. I find myself upset at times thinking of my ex-husband. He is able to have a new relationship, be intimate and free. God asked me, do I really think so? He reminded me about when Peter pointed out about what others were doing, and Jesus said what is it to you what others are doing. Do what I told you to do (John 21:20-22). Why is my focus on others and not on my own assignment? God told me personally to let go. He told me the reason why. So, what am I looking at others for? If I am going to be concerned with anything, I must be concerned about what God told me to do. I was told to let go, but how do I let go?

One day, I was thinking of all I have done against my Father's will in this very room.

Knock knock.

Do I hear knocking?

Knock knock.

I hear knocking yet not on my door.

Knock knock. Mia, can you hear me?

Yes, I can!

Will you let me in?

Father, I am embarrassed. I thought you were already in. Do you not dwell inside of me?

Daughter, I need to get into the secret place of your heart. There seems to be a lock on the door.

Father, what secret place? Forgive me for creating this place unintentionally.

Daughter, walk with Me. Here is the door. It says, "secret sin".

Father, forgive me. Help me to let these things go. I figured I am not hurting anyone. I am not tempting anyone. Just having a little pleasure for the moment. I won't do it all the time. Just enough to keep me from doing the bigger sin.

Daughter, no sin is greater than the other. The wages of sin is death. Is this worth being separated from Me?

No, Father. Why do I feel like I cannot give this up?

Beloved, you are doing it in your own strength. Remember, you can do all things through Christ that strengthens you. No temptation can overtake you. Trust Me to always give you a way of escape.

Father, I have failed many times intentionally. I enjoyed sin. Why?

Daughter, the flesh seeks pleasure and it is fulfilled when he gets what it desires. This is why your desires for the world must change. Once you are transformed by the renewing of your mind by my Word, you will begin to conform to my ways and desire what I desire.

Father, thank you for showing me this place. Can you please help me unlock this place and clean it up, leaving no residue? Help me to not pick up anything to put in this place again. Help me to talk with You about everything so You can deliver me before I try to hide.

May I always be honest about my struggles. May I always be open to receive Your help and guidance. I cannot do this alone, Abba. It's a bit heavy for me. I surrender it all into Your mighty hand. I need you and don't know what I was thinking to act like I don't.

I repent for all my sins. Help me with the desire inside to want it. Kill my flesh daily until it desires the world no more.

Beloved, it is finished. Endure through the process. You shall have what you say, but it's a price you have to pay. It will not be easy, but it will be done. Withstand the test and trials and You shall see My glory. Go and fill this void with My glory, My Spirit and My presence. Think of it no more.

Father, I thank you. I love you. I trust you. Quiet the voices. Be glorified.

Speak to me, Father. Empty me. Maximize my potential. Stir my gifts and manifest them through creativity, visions, ideas, inventions, books, poems and businesses.

Lessons Learned

I refuse to sell my body, peace, or righteousness for the world's help. God told me a storm was coming and that He would be with me. All I have to do is move when He says move. I trust God. I've been here before. He has brought me out, even when I put my hand on some situations. I'm excited to see what my full obedience to my Father gets me. My Abba said He will withhold nothing from me. Take out the laziness, the fear, the comparison and jealous spirits. If there is anything in me that will be a hindrance when I do the job, please remove it all in Jesus' name, Amen. I will walk into my destiny. I will be successful. Poverty is no longer my portion.

No one wants to go through struggles or poverty. Yet, as sure as the seasons change, we must prepare for each one. Invest, save, learn and teach. I was telling my children that we must learn to garden. Gardening and fishing were ways people ate back then. I said, "imagine if — God forbid — we had to live like the Israelites lived back then? Could we survive?" We would have to plant and harvest. No electricity and such. So candles or learning to make fire would need to be learned. Sewing clothes would be needed. I said imagine us having to walk to Belle Isle to go fishing. I'm teaching my children to gain wisdom, adapt and evolve. We shall not crumble or be unprepared ever again when seasons change (Romans 3:25, 8:23).

We understand why people don't prepare for the season's better. It's procrastination. We tend to naturally buy lighter clothes for the summer, an umbrella for the spring, rakes for the fall, and shovel and boots for the winter. Yet, we don't put forth much effort in preparing for the spiritual seasons of life that change. I know some situations are unpredictable, yet to be rooted and grounded in your faith is a priority. Life will not always be happy.

God said in Ecclesiastes 3:1-8 KJV:

To everything there is a season, and a time to every purpose under the heaven: a time to be born, and a time to die; a time to plant, and a time to pluck up that which is planted; a time to kill, and a time to heal; a time to break down, and a time to build up; a time to weep, and a time to laugh; a time to mourn, and a time to dance; a time to cast away stones, and a time to gather stones together; a time to embrace, and a time to refrain from embracing; a time to get, and a time to lose; a time to keep, and a time to cast away; a time to rend, and a time to sew; a time to keep silence and a time to speak; a time to love, and a time to hate; a time of war, and a time of peace.

In knowing this, we must prepare. Natural seasons have a purpose of cycles to make things in life grow, rest, reproduce and pass away. In order for natural seasons to change, there is an alignment and positioning of the earth, sun, and moon. They all must be in position before we feel and see the manifestation of the new season. Within our spiritual lives, we also must get into position and be aligned properly for the changes ahead. God moves when we do our part in aligning ourselves with what He's doing. Getting in position, moving along where He say move, being strong along with praying and seeking Him gets us ready for seasonal changes in our lives. We understand that faith without works is dead. Work is our preparation.

Chapter Six:

Dreams & Visions

My ex-husband realized that God really spoke to me and showed me things in my dreams anytime he was doing something out of order. I approached him about it before I found out through other avenues. He got upset with me one day after dreaming his son had been shot. I instantly prayed, then asked him to pray, but he blew me off. I was considered to be speaking negativity. A few nights later, we received the late-night phone call and he asked if his son was alive. We were both grateful and I glorified God. The situation allowed me to minister to him and let him know God heard my prayers. All glory goes to God.

This chapter includes some of my dreams over the years in no particular order. Hopefully by sharing my dreams, you will begin to see how God not only speaks to me through my dreams, but recognize how He may be speaking to you, as well.

Dream One

I was told continuously to get on this unique elevator whose doors were only a bar to separate the inside from the outside. The elevator was full of rain, but I had to get on it to go up. As it went up, I held onto the bar. In spite of what could happen, I would not let go until I reached the point where the elevator stopped. Elevators only go up and down. As I stepped into the rain on the elevator and held the bar, the elevator went up and began to twirl. It turned upside down and spun me in a circle. I feared the movement almost slipped, but held on for dear life until I reached the floor. I survived, got off the elevator and thanked God.

Revelation: I am in training. There will be unexpected movement, but cover yourself in the washing of the Word of God. That will keep you when nothing else feels adequate.

Dream Two

Inside the house, I went into my bedroom and could see that the window was shattered. It looked like the window was made of Plexiglass; it was shattered yet taped up. I watched as the window heaved in and out as if a wind was blowing, but nothing could get through the window. I fought off what I believed to be spirits that were in the house; however, every time I fought or swung physically, it was a toddler child. The kitchen was the only room that was filled to the roof with water. An aircraft was coming; it was an attack from the enemy. I ran to the basement with the children as I told my older boys to grab their other siblings. We each had to grab someone.

Revelation: The future is uncertain. There are burdens related to intimacy fighting against you. Nourish yourself in the Word of God. The attack will not come as expected. You will need help to protect your lineage.

Dream Three

We each got down to the basement in my childhood home where it had flooded, but there was no water remaining. There was sewer water with the residue of poop and black silt or dirt. To get to a clean spot in the corner, we had to step over the mess. Instead of having a mattress for the younger children to lay on until help arrived, all I had was a blanket. I laid the blanket down and told the children to sit until help arrived. I went back upstairs and went to the mailbox.

We had one mailbox at this house. My mom's mail would be in the front and the others would be in the back. In my dreams, I was randomly getting mail out the box and see checks, letters from prison inmates, court letters and disability letters.

Revelation: The remaining residue of your childhood trauma is of no comfort to your children. You are repeating your mother's pattern instead of providing safe respite.

Dream Four

There was a new thing going on which was laying in bed in the middle of the grocery store. I was the only one doing the new thing. People were debating with me about doing this. After talking to security, I found out they were adding a hotel to the store. As I exited the store, the worker stated this location allowed customers to lay in the bed, but others may not. So, as I spoke with security, I had a pack of family sliced turkey or chicken to make sandwiches with. The guy had paid for his food and took it upstairs. They were so busy debating with me that I got distracted and everyone paid for their food except for me. I had to wait for the others because they had my bridge card. Security asked me was it my card they paid for their food with, and I said yes. He said that I could check the cameras in the system for the card information so I could pay for my meat. It was as if I stood there for an hour. When I finally go to the parking lot, my ride is gone. I went from store to store looking for them. The store had closed, so I was just in the parking lot by myself. The remainder of the dream was with me walking in the parking lot calling and looking for the van.

Revelation: Sharing intimate details in public is temporary for you. Distractions will cause you to lose the very thing you're searching for. Corruption is all around you. This dream was to get your agreement (through payment) for poverty and lack. Remain diligent and focused so there is no confusion in the end.

Dream Five

At an event, I went into the kitchen to help. A church sister who was cooking something special for her husband for Father's Day. Everyone was allowed to taste it, yet when I grabbed one of the cupcake/cookie creations, it became an issue. The piece I grabbed was connected to another piece. I pulled it and the cupcake was connected to another one, so the icing was falling off. She said, "Dang, you took a piece and everything is noticeable!" I tried to walk away from the stove and out the kitchen, but noticed I was squatting up under the counter where the space was very small. I had to attempt three times to crawl out.

I did not let what I saw affect me. In my mind, I entered and was able to get to the sweets, so there had to be a way to get out. As I maneuvered on my feet (imitating how frogs walk but I didn't jump, I walked), I ducked extremely low. I looked up and noticed that under the countertop was all kinds of mess, including icing that had dropped. I said, "Nicole, you get all types of icing under here. She said, "Yeah, I know. My bad." As I came out, there was blue icing in my hair. I asked myself why she made me feel bad for what I did when she made an even bigger mess underneath where no one could see? When I came from under there, I was wearing the icing that she had spilled. I hollered *"It's okay.* I can clean it up." I just pulled the icing out my hair and kept it moving.

Revelation: Coming out will be messy and uncomfortable. Don't think for a moment that others don't have similar messes, it's just theirs is hidden and not public. Keep going anyhow.

Dream Six

I slept well last night. I dreamed of being consecrated to have a committed life of holiness. I also dreamed all my children were gambling at a casino where I had to walk back and forth to teach them. I watched them so they could understand the games they were playing.

Revelation: You may be free of the gambling addiction, but it is not broken off your family. This is a generational curse that must be broken. Don't just sit around living holy and watch them fall into the same mess that you struggled with.

Dream Seven

I dreamed that a storm was coming. It was in the form of a tornado, so me and my children sought shelter. No matter where we were when the storm came, we would be in the basement standing by the furnace. The storm came and moved in a "S" shape. When it came, we ran to whatever location was near to get to their basement. We stood by the furnace to watch the storm move.

At one house, as we stood by the furnace and watched the storm begin to move in the S form, I told the children come on. We had fifteen minutes to get to the next shelter location. When we got outside, my niece's father was in a car waiting out front. He had a bunch of people and a whole lot of stuff in the car, but we got in to hurry to get to our next destination. As he drove, he headed toward an even bigger storm. I looked and it was a forest with the biggest black form around it. I said, "*Oh no!*" We jumped out and ran to the nearest house.

It was a few houses to choose from, but I went to the yellow one. I kicked the door in. I saw some people asleep in bed and looked for their basement. When I went down, the storm came in the basement in the form of a man. I was not afraid as I stood face to face with the man. We talked and a lady came and stood next to him. I looked at her but continued to talk to him.

Revelation: The storm represents your back and forth emotions. The furnace only makes you feel safe because it's warm and comfortable. Confront your emotions and the lives of those it's impacting.

Dream Eight

I dreamed that I was sitting on my bed inside my childhood home. It was a beautiful, sky-blue canopy bed. A baby bear continued to come to my room door. I continued to close the door. All I thought of was that my children were upstairs. The upstairs was my present home. I wondered if they were safe. I prayed they were not coming out of their room so the bear wouldn't attack them. Three of my girls at three different times came downstairs. Each time, I cracked the door open just a little to pull them in so the bear wouldn't get in. I was more scared of letting the bear in without thinking how the girls were able to come downstairs, get in the room and not get attacked. It was as if the bear wanted me, not them.

I saw that the baby bear was not alone. It went from a baby to a bigger bear. The bigger bear walked back and forth as the baby stood at the door waiting to get in. When my baby girl came to get in, I pulled her through the cracked door. For some reason, the baby bear grabbed my right hand and bit it. It wouldn't let go. I hit it continuously against the wall and feared as I did this, the mother bear would get madder as she watched. With pity in my eyes, I prayed it let me go because it was a baby. I didn't want to hurt it, but I definitely didn't want it to hurt me. I shook really hard, it fell off and I shut the door. I opened up the bedroom window and pushed a dresser up against the door. I waited for the bear to push against the door so I could see if the dresser would hold the door so we could get away. As the door was pushed, it didn't budge open so I pushed the three girls out the window and I climbed out.

It was dark outside. In the front of the house, someone's car was running. I got in the car and told them to move over. For some reason, I told them to get my keys and in my truck (the unfamiliar car turned into my truck). I pushed the strangers out my truck and drove off from the past home. Now, I see my childhood home (that is torn down) but in the vision I see the house standing with all the lights on inside, but no curtains on the windows. You can see straight through the house, but it is empty. It was as if when someone cleans a house with the lights are on, and you are able to see through every room.

Revelation: As the baby bear transitioned into an adolescent, that is when he attacked while the mother stood by and watched. Bears are protective like mothers. An aggressive predator, this represents one that has been watching you and your girls waiting to attack. You will consider the person to be innocent, but pay attention to their nature, not their age or size.

Dream Nine

We were being chased. My children and I had to run to the safety of the furnace in the basement. The furnace inside was a huge, circular furnace. It had an area for the children to sit in at the front. The back area was the hot part where the fire came out. I told Zachary (my 16-year-old) don't sit back there with Shalea (my three-year-old baby girl). Sit in the regular space up front so the heat won't burn them. I remember being hidden the first time. The second time we got in, as I sat in front of the furnace, I began to fly around the basement away from the attacker (older, heavyset white man). I remember his focus was trying to hit us with dishes that he had in cupboards all over the basement. It was a wall that I saw (a back wall). I said we got to get him to the brick wall so we could escape. It was the only wall that I saw that lead to the front of the house to get outside.

As we flew around the basement out of his reach, I continued to fly by the wall, so when he threw something it would damage the wall. The man got so mad that when he got close to me, he turned into a giant. As he swung to hit me with his fist, I maneuvered the furnace down so he hit the brick wall and it opened up. A light shone in and birds began to chirp and fly around outside. The giant's face looked defeated as he walked away. As I backed the furnace out the opening, watching the giant get smaller as we escaped from the basement.

Revelation: Do not allow the enemy to outsmart you. When you find your way of escape, he has already lost. Keep going!

Dream Ten

I was driving down a familiar road from previous dreams. It would always have a supermarket outlet with other places on the left and houses on the right with entrance ways further down to turn into railroad tracks, work factories and buildings. Before I got past the houses, my truck broke down. As I waited for help, I turned around to see a crowd of people. It was my ex-husband's family.

"What are y'all doing here?" I asked.

"We live right here." They said.

"Oh my goodness. What a blessing that I am stuck at a place that is safe. You all are family. I can wait here until help comes." I go in the house and my ex-husband's aunt opens the door. I called her Gloria, but it was Aunt Patricia who had gotten killed. I said, "Hi." She had on a red shirt and looked at me wide eyed. I said hey, hugged her and asked if she remembered me. I'm Mia. She said, "yes, Mia; I know." I went in and saw crumbs on the floor. My daughters ate some cornbread. Malia, my six-year-old, was crawling on the table and I made her get down. I begin to clean the floor, moving a huge rug that someone kept pulling over the crumbs. I said, "stop covering the crumbs and pulling the rug." As I swept the cornbread from under the rug, I saw crumbs in the closet. Then cereal wasted, the more I swept. The Cheerios enlarged in size, then trash and shoes appeared. Shoes lined up, but on top of each other - all around messy. Aunt Patricia kept walking by, looking at me as if she was thinking was I really about to try to clean the mess.

Revelation: Cleanse your soul from people you consider safe. They cannot be trusted. Eliminate the chaos.

Dream Eleven

Some horsemen were running down my childhood neighborhood. Every door was open, but as soon as I closed my front door, someone on a bike with four wheels looked, backed up and came to the door. Inside, I was helping a young man with his premature baby as he began to text and get closer. A girl in the text said, "Who is that you are next to?" He said "Mia." She was watching us and he was making it look like we were together. When I checked his phone, he asked why would I check his phone. I said because I saw my name. Then about five ghetto (rowdy) girls came with a gun (bull horn) to my door. I took the bull horn and tried to explain I was only helping him, but they surrounded me so I began to beat them up and surprisingly, they soon fled.

Revelation: You are going against the grain in closing doors that had previously been open to the enemy. Deception is all around you. This is not a carnal war; you must learn to fight in the spirit.

Dream Twelve

The waters of an ocean off a dock opened up. I looked to my left and saw the water standing about twenty feet tall. Dirty water. I was being called onto the ocean floor and as I walked on to the mud, my feet squished but I did not sink. It was a solid foundation. I saw a spot where sea shells were laid. They were a bit dirty, but the Lord said this is where I would find it. I was told to hurry and go back because the waters were about to rise. I rushed back. The water began to rise and hit my feet in splashes of waves as I began to run since I couldn't swim. I had to get ashore in a hurry.

Revelation: The Lord has treasures to reveal. Trust the Lord to find those hidden treasures. Learn to navigate the deep waters of the Word. All God wants to show you is how to receive His breath/Spirit as you surrender your will to Him.

*Dream revelations are provided by the Holy Spirit through Dr. De'Andrea Matthews, author of The Night Season: Unlocking The Mystery Of Your Dreams.

Chapter Seven:
Truth Over Popularity

Four years into my relationship with my ex-husband, I joined a different church and became a faithful member. I wrote the pastor a six-page letter of all I had been through. I laid it all down so he could pray for me to start over fresh. Instead of being welcomed into the fellowship to build relationships, I received awkward looks. My personal business began to float around the church.

One of the deacons, who was married, came by my house to mentor my boys and take them on outings, but he was flirting with me. He asked if it was okay to call me after 9:30 p.m. while already calling me at that time. I talked to a childhood friend who confirmed that he was out of order. Instead of facing it head on, I pulled back from the church altogether. I was very close with the pastor's sister, so I thought I was confiding in her. In actuality, she was getting info from me and spreading it around the church as gossip.

I was invited to my childhood friend's church where they taught straight Bible. It began to pierce me deep where I got so convicted, I knew I needed to change. I was shacking at the time and had gotten pregnant with my first daughter. I couldn't stand the sin, so I told my boyfriend that he had to move in with his sister. It was a battle within because I went from sinning with this man to wanting to live right. It was my life choice that I was pushing on him. That's when God told me this man was an assignment. I used to think God meant my assignment. Not *my* assignment—*an* assignment.

In my church home, there wasn't a strong youth mentorship program. My boys needed strong, faithful, godly men to lead by example. Unfortunately, it is still a need. I desire that my children be saved. I know God does the saving, yet my responsibility as a parent is to protect my children. With my boys, I see that they need men in their lives to teach them what I cannot. As a mother, it's my job to do what I can to find them the help they need.

My boys' Sunday school teachers are a married couple. I approached two brothers in Christ to ask them to talk to my boys about their behavior at home, as well as at school. I walked out of the fellowship hall and saw the brothers.

"Hello, men of God" I greeted. "Can you speak to my boys please?" Then I noticed the wife in the middle. I said, "Hey sis. I did not see you". Then, I walked over and said, "Since I have you both, can you both speak with the boys about their behavior since they are in your classroom?" This was after others inviting me to come to them when needed. I had no problem asking for help or getting better ways to deal with the issues I was having since children sometimes open up to others in confidence. I also asked the teachers if they could please not reward them with any money due to their misbehavior. I stated that if they still wanted to reward them that way, to let me know. She asked me why. I began to tell her how they were acting in a home and in school. I explained they shouldn't be rewarded, knowing they don't give the same effort at school. I explained that ten minutes before church started, they liked to go over the lesson with it fresh on their mind just to get money in class. Other people may not care because as adults I have done this before I took a test. Yet ask me what the answer is now and I cannot tell you.

I am not teaching my children or even living in life myself like this. I teach my children to study to show themselves worthy. Live God's Word. His rewards are greater and unfortunately, the church people did not agree. I don't want my children scanning through God's Word and not realizing the worth because they are focused on the reward of the dollar.

This sister told me home and school life had nothing to do with church. I totally disagree. I teach my children to not live double lives. I hear the excuse, "they are just children." I refuse to believe a child — especially my children, don't know how to act good at all times whether they're in different environments or not. You don't change who you are as a child of God because the environment changes. So, I walked away feeling emotional and offended by my church sister not respecting me or what I asked her about the monetary rewards.

One of our church mothers who paid my boys a few dollars to help clean agreed to hold their funds until the following week. If they are good, they'll receive double. This blessed me because it shows me that we are on one accord. It shows my boys that their actions impact their rewards. The following week, my boys did not get any calls home from school, nor did they get into any fights at home. They changed without me fussing and this is what my focus was.

There was a church meeting because I was offended. The leader who organizes the Sunday school teachers' schedule called for the meeting. The church sister came, but her husband did not. I apologized continuously due to my emotions. The sister asked why was I emotional. I explained to her that I deal with a lot with my boys as a single parent, and I do my best. So when I asked her to be on one accord with me, she chose to tell me I was wrong. Instead of being disrespectful or allowing her to see my face which was showing my emotions, I walked off. She told me that she runs her class and I run my house. I should not have included her in what I do with my children. I could've *asked* her if she had given them any money and it's between me and them if she did give them money. If they chose to be dishonest or not that's her issue.

She then goes to say that I'm out of order for approaching her husband. She says if she's not around don't approach him. I apologized to her. I never want to be disrespectful. She says she not worried about him. Basically, she worried about me and my character around her husband. I had so much to say about that, but chose to pray instead. I am a divorced mother because of a cheating husband who I stayed with a little too long. Why would you think I would attempt to do that to anyone else? That's not my character! Yet I refuse to go back and forth; I will respect her.

The issue for me is I only asked him and the other brothers, who I've known since I have been in the church, to speak in their authority, wisdom, and experience with my boys. This is not the first time I asked them for help. Other men in the church would say okay, try to talk with them but then drop the ball. I believe in asking and not being afraid of the answer.

If I need help, I will ask around until someone helps me find the person who can.

So now that I know her feelings, out of respect, I will not talk to her husband unless they both are together. Isn't that odd that she wants me to respect her as a wife; yet, she doesn't respect me as a mother? This gives me more to pray about. I want to push further. I need to be more focused. This fast will help.

When I was walking in low self-esteem, these same people would offer me clothing but turned out to be insecure and jealous when I started walking confidently. When God started using me to speak a word or minister personally, I got the doubters and rejection from the very ones who have spoken the message over me that God wants to use me, to stop running, to grow up, to mature and to go forth. When I operate in obedience to God, you rollin' your eyes at me. I just pray to love past all of this.

With church hugs, I am avoided or hugged partially and I can feel the disconnection. I notice a different interaction between others and myself. God had showed me that I was a people pleaser and I have to pray to love as God purposed. I will understand the difference between loving people and pleasing them. My assignment is to love them and please

God. I trust God to teach me how to love people and with loving people correctly I am pleasing God. And if you are like me, when you are loved right, it is sure to please you. I just want and desire to love people right.

An Inbox of Admiration

A young lady requested me as a Facebook friend, and I accepted it. She then inboxed me to say how she admires my love for the Holy Spirit. I responded by giving God the glory. I told her I love God and the Holy Spirit, and even in my imperfections, I ask God to use my life as a testimony to glorify Him. People are watching what we say and how we live. Our reactions to life situations. I do not ever want to be a person who claims Christ to make myself appear to be saved.

When people look at me, I want them to actually see God. I will never be perfect, yet they will see God dwelling inside. They won't see me in all my emotions. Even being human, emotional, and imperfect people can easily see the glory of God. I want the first image people see in me to be God. I want God to continuously use me as an influencer to draw His people near. I want to continuously be humble even in my struggles. Always being aware that people are watching. I want to labor and serve for the kingdom and ministering in areas where needed.

At my next church as the pastor taught Bible study and was prophesying, he said, "We are one decision away from living the life God has for us." He read from Psalm 121 and 2 Peter 1:4. After class, pastor asked to speak with me in his office. He told me God said, "Hurry Up." He said he saw someone in the church try to do something to one of my children. He stated he didn't know what is going on, yet I need to listen to God and move when He says move.

I told him about my dream and he gave me the exact interpretation that Dr. Matthews had given to me. What blew my mind is he described the very basement from my dream. The exact location of the stairs, the furnace and the brick wall leading to the front of the house. I hollered. How could he see what I dreamed? He said it was playing like a movie as I told him. The Lord continued to speak to me.

Pastor stated that was the first time in a while someone told him a dream and he could see it play out. I don't know how to feel. I feel happy, excited and at a place of urgency to know what God wants to do. I want to be obedient. I want to get life right. I don't want to mess up or act nonchalant about my purpose. I don't want to be distracted. *Lord, be it unto me what You desire, will and purpose to do in and through me. In Jesus' name. Amen.*

I kept having dreams of my past leaders rejecting me as I tried to find the right church home. I just want to get healed in my emotions. Why so much rejection? It hurts because I love them. Am I having the dreams because they told me God didn't tell *them* about me leaving? Or are they feeling rejected themselves? Lord, help me be okay regarding each decision. I am not lacking any love in the new ministry. My spiritual parents received me and my children with open arms. I am at peace in my spirit. Glory to God.

God is amazing. He has a way of changing your heart and helping you love people on a different level. Have you ever tried to love someone who hurt you, abused you or neglected you? It's hard being rejected. It's hard knowing our God requires us to love those we know are considered to be enemies. So, how do you love them? I always focus on the root to know when it is the enemy. It is a spirit that works within them. So, I pray against it as I allow God to work within me.

We can identify the spirit that is working in us, we just have to be honest. When I get an attitude and have these negative thoughts, I know it is the enemy. Sometimes, I get so fed up with people that I choose not to pray to get over the issue. I intentionally choose to dwell on it and let the anger rise. My flesh is satisfied, and I think I'm winning by being mad and showing them I am not a pushover. Yet, we all know the flesh is never satisfied. If you add fuel to the fire, it will continue to burn. This is where disunity and unforgiveness occurs. No one wants to humble themselves. Pride has taken root and taken over.

Lesson Learned

These are the issues that are sure to occur if you rebel against the Spirit of God. God is trying to show us how to love through every situation. There are levels of love. Who knew? The same people in my life who commend me as a good parent could be the same ones who are not on one accord with the decisions I make to discipline my children.

God will always warn you of people's motives and intentions even when you are in sin. God will still love you enough to show you people's character and give you free will to walk the straight and narrow path or continuously wallow in sin. *Abba Father, thank you for loving me, showing me and warning me of the destruction. Keep me preserved. Grow me up and past this situation. Help me to surrender and let go fully. I surrender, Lord.*

Chapter Eight:
Hearing God

When I first heard God call me to live right, I was twenty-six years old. I had five children, all boys. I began to go to church and read the Bible regularly. I would show up to church early and sit out front so I wouldn't be late. I had been dealing with my ex for fifteen years, seven of those years as my husband. The more he mistreated me and cheated, the more I ran to God. In the midst of all my sin, I desired to live a holy life.

I get so many inboxes and messages from people who say they admire me and that I am an inspiration. *Who me? Mia with eleven children? Mia, who is divorced but can't seem to let go fully of a man who is not for her? Mia, who is fat and can't seem to get it together? Mia, who lives in a crumbling house with mice and roaches?* I said all of this to myself, but it was words spoken by other people. Were these actually my thoughts, or was I holding onto other's opinions of me? My self-esteem was so low that I began to walk like it.

We were connected to so many people who blessed us with gas fare, clothing and food…anything their heart desired to bless us. I have never been in a position of overflowing blessings like this. I usually have been the one giving and the people took advantage. It's hard to know how to receive with no ill intent, so I would try to find a way to repay someone. I am accustomed to dealing with people who expected me to overcompensate whenever I borrowed something or needed them. However, when I changed my circle and showed the same behavior, it offended them. I was continuously told they do it to help, not to be compensated. Glory to God. I had a hard time believing people had hearts like mine. I am not the only one.

Those feelings became overwhelming, so I wanted to hold onto everyone and love them forever. I am told I can be overbearing. I don't have to tell people I love them. Love in my life came with conditions. I love you, but I will kill you if you leave me. I love you, but I'm cheating on you. I love you, but I don't want to be bothered with you (rejection).

Lord, let me love people the right way. Give me a chance to love them and mean it. Love them not only with my words, but with my hands to bless, my feet to walk with them and be supportive and my ears to listen to their heart's cry (their emotions). Father, let me be there to minister to their need no matter how long it takes. Let me unconditionally love your people. Let me look past what they are doing, saying and even smelling like. Lord, let me see in your children what you see. Let me love them wholeheartedly.

God did just that. I love everyone with a godly love and I don't know how to turn it off. I have encountered people who have talked about me, stolen money from me, lied on me, yet I still love them and wouldn't want to see any harm come to them. People have filed my children on their taxes and stole money. I was scared, yet I believe we reap what we sow sooner or later. Not reacting the way people expect when they mess over you is itself a blessing.

I used to love to fight, and still would not have a problem defending mine; yet God says He will fight our battles and vengeance is His. So, when people do me wrong, I have no issue explaining what I would do in the flesh, but I make sure to let them know that God will handle them. People tend to take advantage of God's longsuffering and patience. God will have His way with His people in His due time. Don't rush it, thinking you're ready. God's wrath can be unquenchable, so don't mock Him.

One friend I was close to became verbally abusive. She was dealing with issues of being bipolar. So many times she would flip out on me. Go and tell my personal business and talk about me being stupid for staying with my husband, and how my house smelled like pee. I was having trouble with my boys; she even said they gonna end up in jail or dead. I bound up all those word curses spoken against my children, yet I continued to be her friend. I refused to walk away from her due to a condition I believe she had no control over. Things just didn't get any better. She continued to be verbally abusive. I was tired of being talked about from people she told my business to. It got so bad that a guy she was dating told my husband's sister's friend that he slept with me. Why? I don't know that man. This became the beginning of fights with my husband and him calling me a liar.

My ex-husband ended up cheating because he thought I had. He claimed the guy said he was with me and I told him to have the guy call me to confirm. I was really sarcastic, asking things like, "What I look like naked? How did we have sex? When? Where? What time? Don't play with me or lie on me." Yet, it was too late. This became the beginning of fights with my ex-husband and him calling me a liar.

My husband, family and friends were all over the internet calling me a whore, talking about I'm not saved. I personally went to the girl and asked her why would he say that. How did my name come up? I told her I only seen him when I was with my friend. This is the guy who abused her. I asked her many questions, and yet I told her that the truth will come out. When the truth comes out, then will you know my truth.

Later, my husband and his people approached the guy who admitted to lying. Yet, my husband still questioned his motives. I was still thought to be a cheater. God showed me that friendship had run its course. God also showed her because a week later at church, she came to me crying, saying God showed her our friendship was over. She cried and said, "I don't want to lose you." I told her, "I love you, yet your dream was confirmation." I was like, *Wow. God, You showed her, too.*

Why do we fear the barren time?

I believe it's more of a "don't want to deal with the barren times." I questioned how some people crumbled when losing a job. It was because I come from a place where I always was low income. I didn't have the expensive clothes or cars. Being low income got food from various places where I was unashamed to stand in lines and eat whatever was given. Whether I liked it or not, food was food. I had to live without electricity and gas. I had to catch the bus or walk to my destinations. I grew up in the barren time so I couldn't relate to those who lived well. Now, as I receive God and He is raising me up and pulling me out my place of complacency, I have to learn to adapt to living my best life.

Crazy right? I was used to sitting at home; now, I am pushed to go out and fellowship. I was used to not affording, but now God wants me to be able to afford it. Many people wouldn't like to struggle, yet I was at a place where that was my survival tactic. I had mastered the struggle. I could help you survive a famine because I had already done so.

Many people would come to me to ask privately where to go to get different resources and I would gladly direct them. I would always inform them to be consistent because sometimes people treat you different when you are in need. Although that is not fair, it is a very humbling place. People in positions tend to take advantage of their authority and can make you feel so ashamed. I would offer to go with them because I am unashamed and sometimes, the support of another while you are going through helps and encourages you.

My daily routine consisted of early morning prayer. I would go pray at 4 a.m., then take my children to prayer from 5:30 p.m. to 6:30 p.m. It was the summer, so I would stop at the park for a few minutes just to allow them to run around. We mainly would go to church and go home. I probably smothered them in fear of losing them. I had to understand that God saved all of our lives so why did I not trust Him to continue to keep us?

During a corporate church fast, I fasted and prayed to be delivered from those things I need to be loosed from, particularly the soul tie with my ex-husband. I need insight and understanding so I can study and teach the Sunday school lessons. I want to obtain all the knowledge to succeed with the training for Intuit Turbo Tax so I can work from home. I also pray for balance and self-control.

God amazes me how quickly He turns a situation around when you begin to walk in it while not even realizing it. I could never imagine myself fasting without eating and not be hungry. I had to smile. It feels good to be led by God and reap the benefits. I have to fight off the lies of the enemy, saying, "You're only fasting to lost weight." *Do you even understand? Why are you even talking to me? You will not distract me. You will not discourage me. The more I deny my flesh, all you try to use fleshly against me will quiet your voice the more. My God told me to seek first His kingdom and His righteousness, and all else will be added. As I humble myself and pray, turning from my wicked ways as well as fasting (denying myself), God will be glorified. I will not be distracted. Jesus, I welcome You and the Holy Spirit. Quiet the mouth of the enemy. Lord, be glorified.*

Many friends were an ear yet had issues of their own. I confided in whomever had an ear to listen and that was unwise. I turned to many people throughout my life to help me. I had to deal with people rejecting me because my past was too much, people taking advantage because my love for people and desire to please them was too much. My business was always in the streets or negatively spreading throughout the church through gossipers because my mouth told it all.

Someone told me one day to stop putting the bullets in the gun for someone to shoot me. After being hurt so many times, I became numb and started to not care. This is just the way life is. No matter who I talk to, thinking they are for me and they never are. One day, I met my best friend, Hope Mills. We have been close for almost six years. I can honestly say she's closer to me than my biological sister. We already been going to church together but we just never hung out. It took for us both to be hurt by a mutual friend for us to connect. I thank God for her. Although neither one of us are perfect, the divine connection from God is so evident. Our spirits seem to recognize their own.

Hope came into my life at the point when I was trying to divorce my ex-husband. She didn't give up on the friendship because I stayed in my dysfunctional marriage. She didn't get tired of talking to me and ministering to me when I was hurt. She didn't run when I needed her. She was not embarrassed by what I looked like. She helped me build my self-esteem. She showed me how to love myself a little more. She held on to me like a sister should.

Many said I was too dependent on her, yet nobody knew I had to hold onto her at the moment as God allowed so I wouldn't sink. I was dying spiritually and on the verge of suicide naturally. I had stopped taking care of myself. I was tired of friends leaving me. I was tired of being controlled and used. Hope came into my life and made me be independent. Instead of me always doing what others wanted, being a "yes girl" doing whatever they wanted me to do, Hope pushed me to make choices on what and where I wanted to go, do and eat. My life began to change.

I began to heal from low self-esteem when I was shown how to take care of myself, which didn't cost a lot. I began to walk in confidence and not be so depressed. I had someone to talk to who didn't tell my business. If she did tell anyone, she would call to say, "Hey Sister. I'm about to tell your business." It was always as a testimony to encourage and bless another. This sisterhood and friendship definitely healed me from rejection and low self-esteem. I don't listen to people anymore when they try to talk negatively. Sisterhood was needed.

I can tell Hope anything and she will respond in two ways—first, as my sister and friend, then she will give me exactly what God wants her to give me. It feels so good to have a friend who is not so heavenly bound that she is no earthly good. She does not beat me up with scripture, yet she ministers to me with God's Word.

I tell her all the time how I know being my friend is not easy. Especially when I was going through after the fire—depressed, lazy, with low self-esteem, bitter and irritable because I was pregnant. She told me, "Girl, I was gonna tell God let me slap her but still be her friend." The things I was doing required some sense being slapped into me. I was at such a low place. I became extra lazy. I called my children to do everything and she continued to tell me I'm going to make the baby I'm carrying lazy. I knew I could not keep waking my children up, having them do everything. I was so lazy that I did not do anything to myself as far as my appearance, especially my hair. I have some cute wigs, yet those days I did not want to wear them.

Between November 2015 and July 2016, Hope would do my grocery shopping for me every month during my pregnancy. She definitely is one of a kind. Although she disliked how I was treated in my marriage, she was always respectful when he was around. This was a blessing to me. She helped me so much emotionally, and she has wisdom in many areas. She used to tell me all the time when I was married that she cannot give me any advice because she is not married. She can only relate to the relationship's comparable issues. I told her I understand, yet her testimony itself helps.

When she found out I won this contest to write my first book, she celebrated me not by just words but action. She took me to dinner, wherever I wanted to go. No one has ever celebrated me like that and she did it just because. We don't have the perfect relationship because I know I get on all of her nerves at times. I have my share of days when I roll my eyes at her. It is all in love. A God-ordained relationship.

Her character is so pure though. We have our share of attacks from the enemy. He tried to divide us with jealousy, but God. God has prophesied three times about how we would minister together. We have been tested. We also had to deal with periods of separation. We were too close at one point and God said we were too dependent on each other. He didn't want us calling each other before we talked to Him. He wanted us to talk to Him first, then call each other.

God is a jealous God. We must put no one before Him. We have that understanding now. To build with each other, we must build our relationship as God states. He must come first. There is so much I can say about my Hope. She definitely is a friend, sister, confidante. Jesus said show yourself friendly. I am grateful to call her a friend. It's a blessing to have a friend/sister to make life worth living.

Chapter Nine:

My Testimony

What was my life like before I met Jesus?

After listening to a Myles Munroe's sermon regarding the Holy Spirit being the most important person on Earth, I began to understand clearly that my life as I've known it was never my own. God had plans for me before He even formed me in my mother's womb. I had lived a life of sin, and in sin created a history of issues of life that were not God-led. God was always watching, in spite of my paths I chose. He was waiting on me to tap into *who I really am*. When would I learn who I was? My life without Jesus was void and I was just existing. Going through life meaningless and not accomplishing much.

It seems whenever I did succeed, it sooner or later would crumble and I had to start again either with the same thing or trying something different. A common cliché was every time I take a step forward, I get knocked two steps back. I remember praying and asking God, *what am I doing wrong*? I believe God was telling me everything—*follow me, obey me*. That's what God was calling me to do. Why was that so hard for me? I was a people pleaser and that was a big problem with seeking a relationship with God. Now, I realize I needed Jesus.

No matter what I did, said, purchased, or agreed to with people, I never satisfied them. I went my whole life doing what people asked. Sacrificing my time and money. Loving beyond their flaws and yet I always got hurt. I began praying even at a young age for answers. Why was my heart so big? Why am I not receiving the same energy and love back that I give out? Why are people hurting me? I had all these questions and Jesus had all the answers.

It took years for me to get this revelation. As I learned to open up and let Jesus in my heart, I realized how much I needed Him and can't live without Him. He fills the voids I have always felt. He is my way to our Father. There I can be at a place of rest in my mind and receive all I need and desire spiritually. I have always had these mind battles and knowing that God can and will fight with and for me. I receive such a peace where I am no longer all over the place. This was a big issue for me. There was an attack on my sanity and I needed God more than ever. Now, I know that in everything, I need Jesus.

How I committed my life to Jesus

After leaving Bible class, I was reminded of how my life has changed. I had been to other churches before and have heard great preachers, too. I had never heard or experienced being part of a ministry that prayed daily at the church, though. It was something that I desperately needed from my church leaders.

The bishop taught straight Bible, baptized in Holy Ghost fire, fasted and prayed among many more truths of God. When God told the bishop that he was to come to the church daily to pray, I jumped right on board. My children and I went to the temple to pray together; other days, I went alone. I started fasting monthly with the ministry. Some months, I couldn't and some I didn't do the complete three days; yet the majority of the time I would. God is so faithful. He still honored my desire and sacrifice when I did fast. The difference Jesus made in my life from my heart desire to be obedient was life-changing.

My eyes opened as I gained a clearer understanding of who God is. The more I prayed, the more God talked to me and showed me dreams. Even now, I cry with an urgency in my spirit because God shows me people in my dreams. Many times, there are secrets that they are dealing with, which nobody knows about. I ask God, *what do you want me to do with this information?* I used to Google what my dreams mean. I learned God shows us things in dreams to encourage, uplift, and even bring warning. My life has changed when I realized this was a gift because I am held accountable for what I see. God has a purpose for me. I love that God is walking with me. There is no greater love than this.

What help did I seek to get healed?

God told me to just tell the story. I said, "Lord I want the readers to be more focused on You bringing me out than the story of my experiences." He told me to just write it unashamed and that He will get the glory. Many times, we don't open up in fear of people's responses. That is not our concern when we tell our testimony. God will reach whom He wants to reach and He will cover us from the persecution and judgment of the others.

Jesus warned us that we will be persecuted for righteousness sake (Matthew 5:10 KJV). He said we would become afraid of the testimony due to its sin and imperfection. Remember no man is perfect. Your testimony is being told to help others come out or walk through because you have done it. I have a saying to people when they bring up my past. *Jesus, this is for you.* Give that conversation right to Jesus because your past is no longer your concern. That is over and when a person brings up your past, then they definitely need Jesus to transform their thinking.

The Bible says a man taking to the plow and looking back is not fit for the kingdom of God. Jesus demonstrated looking to the future. He died for our sins so we may be saved and said, " It is finished." He didn't say *almost* finished. The very man on the cross who got crucified with Jesus had past sins. Although he was crucified, upon confirming who Jesus was, he confirmed a seat with Christ in Heaven. All the man had to do was believe and confess with his mouth that Jesus is the son of God (Romans 10:9).

I was so worried about people remembering what I went through, I did not even begin to understand that personal stories were easier to relate to than principles. People love to hear stories, especially if it captures their attention. With my testimony, I pray to reach believers and nonbelievers. Unbelievers would probably lose interest if I started quoting scriptures. We all have a natural curiosity of experiences we never had. Sharing helps Jesus walk into their hearts as we share personal narratives.

I have always been a transparent person. I never hid my struggles, failures or most importantly, my faith in God. Many people felt I talked too much because with transparency came negativity, yet God continued to tell me to keep sharing. Periodically, I would get personal messages from those needing advice, wanting to talk and needing prayer. Once, I was asked to come pray and bless her house. I had just had a miscarriage after getting pregnant by my ex-husband. I told her I couldn't do that. I was not a pastor. I had just fornicated. I could not pray and bless her house. It was not what I was *ordained* to do. She told me that God has forgiven me and my purpose has not changed because I have sinned. I asked for forgiveness and repented knowing it was done.

I felt so horrible. I chose to dwell in my failures and not join together in faith for God to cover her home. I had to repent for that very thought. How can I have so little faith in my Abba Father who hears my prayers all because I fell? That's how we are in our relationship with God. We devalue our worth and purpose due to the mess.

Just as a newborn baby is born with purpose, from infancy to adulthood, there are stages of growth and what is required at each stage. Toddlers are required to be toilet trained. Upon being toilet trained, if they make a mess, we discipline in appropriate ways to show the child that they were wrong, yet we clean them up and redirect them on what to do better.

When God told me to move, it was to be done in His timing. I had to sacrifice and not dwell on or procrastinate on moving. I had to not try to figure it out on my own. When God spoke, He expected me to trust Him as I followed. I honestly I told myself that I would trust God to keep us.

God saw the bigger picture when I didn't. God would never speak without reason and purpose. If God said to do something, there is always a reason behind it. We don't always have to understand it at that moment. God will, in due time, give you the understanding you need. Obedience is better than sacrifice (1 Samuel 15:22).

Chapter Ten:

God Gets the Glory

God gets the glory in my life. In spite of being molested, I am still able to love through the pain. I thank God the pain didn't cause me to walk continuously in brokenness. I am not repeating the same thing done to me. I am not confused about my sexuality. I trust God that the generational curse is broken and will not pass to my other children. I thank God I am in my right mind and not fearful of it happening, yet being watchful for the signs so I can protect my children. I thank God I know how to pray specifically about this issue so I can intercede to bind and cast down that perverse spirit.

God gets the glory in my life because although I was in a domestic violence situation, I can still stand and recognize that I am beautiful. My Abba tells me I am fearfully and wonderfully made. I am the apple of His eye. He loves me and everything about me. I do not have to walk around with low self-esteem. I was uniquely created for purpose. Although man may not have understood me, God wants to show me my purpose. I thank God that I am able to still love and recognize love is not supposed to hurt in that way. Although I am divorced, I am not rejected. There is a man of God for me. I thank God that I can desire to be married and not be afraid of failure. In my waiting, I thank God that He is preparing me and teaching me His ways so I know what to look for.

God gets the glory that in spite of my poverty situation, I learned to trust and have faith in Him. God takes care of His own. I can say without a doubt God provided when we needed or even wanted something. All we had to do was ask in faith, and God moved on our behalf. Bills were overdue, yet God made a way where I could pay what I had or seek help to get funds to keep the utilities on. My truck was not the best, yet God made sure in spite of it needing repair, I was able to get to and from my destinations. Even when it broke down, I was able to call on someone.

Many may say travesty is human nature or to be expected. No, it's not. I can call on those in time of need and they will be unavailable to help. Strangers can ride by and not attempt to stop. God will put me on an unexpected person's heart who is not on my call list to ask for help. They can call me just to say God put you on my heart and that will be an open door to receive the help God intended. I will receive and the person sent will also receive. These situations will always be an elevation of faith for me. True to the Word of God, He has a ram in a bush. God is awesome. Where He guides, He provides. I have never been forsaken by God, even when I didn't recognize His presence.

You ever encounter people who question or complain "Why me?" when situations take place? Most importantly, have *you* been that person who questions God asking why me? There may be so much truth to the unfairness. As I look at what I've endured, some people have gone through worse than what I've been through. Many people believe what they endured is not as bad as what I went through. We can exchange stories; nevertheless, I don't believe in comparing. God never puts more us than we can handle. Every person's storms are different. Even when we don't understand why we deal with issues at the hands of others. I always look at what Jesus did for us all for the purpose of us seeing the kingdom of God.

What about the people who don't know about Jesus? My response is that everyone shall know and hear about Jesus because it is our assignment as believers to go to the nations to tell of His goodness. His story. His testimony. Jesus paid the price for our salvation so we can be saved. We were bought with a price, so we must pay a price as well. No more dying on a physical cross, yet we have to die daily. We must surrender our life to Christ. Receive His blood in exchange for our flesh. We must give up the old man which we were born into and receive the newness of Christ. A worthy price to pay and not easy but we can do all things through Christ who strengthens us.

Spreading the gospel in these times has become easy and convenient because we have the internet that reach places we cannot physically visit. If we chose to focus on the reasons something is happening and try our best to not focus on what is happening, we can begin to see God's glory. This is indeed the hardest thing to do in our human nature. Is help indeed available for those going through? Yes. If you look around and document issues that are going on in the world. document if there is a solution. If there is not, do you believe you have one? Why or why not? It is so much I see and have ideas yet I believe money, transportation or even knowing where to start are the issues. We cannot help the whole world, but we can help the world by helping one individual at a time. I know that pain is a huge issue to deal with.

We live in a world in which the enemy has control. We must remember that greater is He that is in us, than He that is in the world. We must cast those spirits down. You may be saying, *what about the innocent youth who may not know how to pray?* Do you believe your prayers are answered and heard?

If we do our part and join together to pray and bind up the spirits and release the fruit of the Spirit from God, I believe change will take place. We have work to do; but through it all, God gets the glory.

Epilogue

Compiling my autobiography has taken a number of years. Since the first draft, several things have changed for the better. I am completely delivered from my prior addictions of masturbation and gambling. My three oldest children are adults and living on their own. That leaves me with eight children currently at home. I am also no longer attending the churches mentioned; however, my relationship with God is stronger than ever.

I am overjoyed to share my story with you as a first-time author and would love to hear from you. Feel free to connect with me on social media at Mia Tillman on Facebook. Thanks in advance.

About the Author

Humble, compassionate, and spirit-filled, Mia Tillman isn't a stranger to misfortune. As one who pursues an intimate relationship with God as Father, Mia stands on the word of God as her strength in the continual stride to be the best mother possible to her eleven children. After dropping out of high school due to teen pregnancy, Mia received her GED and went on to receive her medical assistant diploma from the National Institute of Technology a year later. Now licensed as a certified nurse aide, Mia's greatest accomplishment has been raising her seven boys and four girls. Mia aspires to inspire all with her success story of surviving financial hardship, homelessness and divorce while trusting God to save, deliver and sanctify her and her children.

Thank you for supporting authors from diverse communities. Feel free to email MsMiaLashawnTillman@gmail.com for media requests or interviews.

CPSIA information can be obtained
at www.ICGtesting.com
Printed in the USA
LVHW100738260422
717138LV00006B/195

9 781954 274907